BOOK ONE

The Secret Oath

BOOK TWO

The Secret of Coral Cave

BOOK THREE

The Poachers

EDITOR'S NOTE:
Each of these books is entirely fictional, with any resemblance to actual people or happenings completely coincidental.

THE RUGENDO RHINOS

AND

CHAPTER ONE

The Tree House

We entered the thick forest following a path that snaked its way between the giant trees. The path, actually an animal trail, had been made by dik-diks, small rabbit-size antelope, that raided our cabbage patch. We carried air rifles and stalked quietly down the path using our gun barrels to push aside overhanging ferns. We were the Rugendo Rhinos going on a hunting hike.

Rugendo Rhinos is the name of our club. We hadn't chosen the name Rugendo. It happened to be the name of the mission station where we lived in the Kenya highlands. Rugendo meant "journey" in the local language, and many missionary trips or safaris had started out from Rugendo. We had picked the name Rhinos for our club because it started with an "R" like Rugendo. And our club was in Africa where rhinos live. I remember the day we started the club.

There were four boys in the fifth and sixth grades who lived at Rugendo. Our parents worked as missionaries and we were "M.K.s," or missionary kids. First there was Matt Chadwick. His dad taught African pastors and his mom was a nurse. Matt was like a Thomson's gazelle's tail. He could never stop moving. He always had to be doing something, like chasing a honey guide bird through the forest to see where the bee hive was or playing soccer or catching and frying peanut-flavored flying ants. We were never bored with Matt around. And because of his enthusiasm we accepted him as our leader. It had been his idea to build a tree fort and use it as the headquarters for our club.

I love doing things as much as Matt, but I'd rather follow his suggestions than decide what to do. After all, someone might not like my ideas. My name is Dean Sandler and the day Matt suggested we build a tree fort I backed him all the way. He said we should build a tree fort in the big wild fig tree in the ravine. It was the kind of tree where the Kikuyu people used to worship their gods before the missionaries came and taught them about Jesus.

"It'll be more than a tree fort," Matt said. "It will be a tree castle. We'll build ten rooms. Why, I'll bet we can build a tree house like the Swiss Family Robinson tree house I saw at Disneyland last year when our family was in the United States on furlough."

"Yeah, it'll be great," I chimed in.

At that point, the third member of our group, Dave Krenden, spoke up. Dave's dad worked as a builder and right then he was constructing a new wing on the mission hospital. Dave, tall and thin, loved helping his dad at building sites and had learned a lot. "Hold on a minute," Dave said in his slow, methodical way. "We can't build a ten-room tree house just like that. It'll take planning. We'll have to use the right kind of boards and build supports or the whole thing will collapse."

Matt hadn't thought about that. Neither had I. But Dave had. It's good to have a guy like Dave if you ever have a club. Dave wanted to see the tree. "After I see the tree," Dave said, "I should be able to draw up some plans with my dad's help."

We set off at once for the wild fig tree. Jon Freedman, the fourth member of our group, led the way. Jon was an explorer. He loved hiking, hunting, and trapping. He had only one fault. He became impatient with the rest of us when we stumbled into wait-a-bit thorns and started yelling and scaring off our prey and other little things like that. He expected each of us to be a mini-Tarzan as he was. His parents, both doctors, had come to Rugendo the year before. They had worried that Jon would miss TV when they took him away from America. Now they wondered whether Jon would ever leave Africa. Jon's sole ambition in life was to become a big-game hunter.

Jon barged through the bushes that day, opening a trail for the rest of us to follow. The tree stood astride a deep ravine about a mile from Rugendo. When we got there we climbed all over the tree with its massive branches and free-hanging roots. We pointed excitedly to where we'd build various rooms. Dave, though, quietly pondered while we frolicked. I saw his forehead wrinkle in concentration.

Just then Jon let out a whoop as he grasped a vine and pushed himself off the tree. He swung out over the ravine and back again. "Hey, guys, this is great," he called. Matt and I shinnied up to join him. Dave stood on the ground and walked around the trunk of the tree, nodding to himself.

"What do you think, Dave?" Matt yelled down. "Can we build a tree fort?"

Dave looked up and smiled. "Well, Matt, it won't be a ten-room castle. But I think we can build a solid two-room tree house."

"Hey, we can have a club," said Matt. "A secret club, and this can be our clubhouse."

"Sounds great," I said. "This will be super! Our own secret clubhouse!"

The other two had agreed. Right there in the branches of the wild fig tree we had formed the Rugendo Rhinos. Matt had been the one who said Rhinos sounded good with Rugendo, so the Rhinos we became.

It took a week of hard work to build the tree house and Dave's dad insisted on inspecting it before he would let us use it. We didn't want our parents to know where our tree fort was. How can you have a secret club-house when everyone knows how to find it?

Dave's dad approved of the tree house. We could see he was proud of Dave. But he also knew we wanted the location of our tree house to be a secret. So, after inspecting our work, he gathered us around and said in a low voice, "Now that I know it's safe, I have no idea where I am or how I got here. In fact, I think I'm having an amnesia attack. Could you boys please direct me to the Rugendo mission station?" Then he winked at us. We all grinned. We knew our secret would be safe with him. We guided him back to Rugendo.

In our first club meeting, we elected Matt captain of the Rhinos. I had been elected secretary because I got good grades in English. I didn't tell anyone about the bad grades I got in handwriting. I figured if I could read what I'd written, it really didn't matter if it was poorly written. Unfortunately, there were many times when I *couldn't* read what I had written. My dad edited a Christian magazine for Africans and my mom was a secretary at the magazine office, so all my friends figured I'd make a good secretary. I was honored, even though I wasn't sure what I was supposed to do.

We voted Dave in as treasurer. Since he was so careful in everything he did, we thought he'd be careful with our club's money. Of course we didn't have any money. But we said we'd make up club rules and have dues and things.

Jon didn't get elected to anything. We didn't know about any other positions, so he became our member. He was so busy planning our hunting trips he didn't even notice.

That's how we became the Rugendo

Rhinos. Now, as we slipped into the forest, we were going on an all-Rhino pigeon hunt. We each had a pocket full of pellets and an air rifle. Actually, Jon carried his pellets under his tongue. "Easier to get out quickly," he told us one day. What he said was true. I can still remember trying to get pellets out of my pocket in the heat of a hunt and having difficulty pulling them out from among the candy wrappers, dried gum, black pieces of volcanic glass, and various other treasures that filled my pockets. But I worried that pellets in the mouth could give me lead poisoning, so I kept my ammo in my pocket, despite the difficulties.

Jon led the way as usual. We came to a grassy glade in the middle of the forest. Jon spotted the pigeon first. We called them pigeons. My dad was a bird watcher and he had told me the correct name was ring-necked dove. I had brought this up at one of our club meetings. Everyone agreed we should call our quarry by its proper name. But when we hunted, we always slipped back and called them pigeons.

"There's the pigeon," Jon whispered. "It just landed in that wild olive tree over there."

I could see the tree with its scaly bark and

pale green-gray leaves. But I couldn't see the bird. I whispered this fact to Matt who smiled and said, "I can't see it either. That's why I have Jon lead our hunts." I nodded wisely.

We inched forward to within twenty yards of the tree. Then I saw it—the plumpest ring-necked dove I'd ever seen. I pointed at it and whispered, "I see it!" At that moment it flew into the air, wings flapping loudly. Jon gave me a nasty look. I felt terrible. But before I could even apologize, Jon had swung his head and was following the flight of the bird.

"Okay, it's landed again," Jon said. "Now this time, let's be quiet and avoid any sudden movements."

"My lips are sealed," I said, making a zipping motion across my mouth. "I'm sorry about scaring the pigeon."

Jon scowled and began stalking the bird again. Matt followed him. But Dave patted me on the shoulder. "It's okay," he whispered. "We all make mistakes. I hadn't even seen the pigeon yet when you spoke up and scared it."

Dave had a way of helping a guy feel better and I smiled my appreciation to him.

This time I was extra quiet as we followed

Jon. Jon silently led our stalk on the fat pigeon or dove or whatever that gray bird was called. Jon wanted to call it supper. When we got close enough, Jon leaned his gun in the crotch of a branch in a low bush and aimed. But before he could squeeze the trigger, the bird again flew up in a flurry of flapping wings.

This time it hadn't been me who had spooked the bird. It was a Kikuyu man, dressed in traditional animal-skin clothing. He shuffled down the path to our left. He had gray hair and carried a goatskin bag in one hand and a squirming kid goat under his other arm. We watched as he hurried past without noticing us. Then he was gone.

"I wonder who that was?" Matt asked.

"He looked like a witch doctor," I answered. The others laughed at my imagination.

"Well, let's get on with the hunt," Jon reminded us. "That pigeon will be eaten tonight. See that tree over there?" We stalked the bird again. This time the bird flew before we got near enough to aim.

"Let's take a break," Matt suggested. We sat down under a tree, unbuckled our canteens and drank.

As we sat resting, Dave heard the sound

first. "What's that noise?" he asked.

"The noise is you talking," Matt answered, laughing at his own wit.

"No, I'm serious," said Dave. "Listen."

We listened. Then I heard it. "It sounds like a drum," I said. "BOM-tum-tum-BOM-tum-tum-BOM, like that."

Matt and Jon heard it too.

"I wonder what it is?" Dave asked again.

"Let's find out," Matt said.

"What about the pigeons?" Jon asked.

"We'll hunt them later," Matt answered.

This time Matt led the way. We would walk for a while, then stop and listen to be sure we were heading in the right direction. We soon found the path the old man had been on. We found it easier to walk on the path than to keep bush-barging. Besides, the sound seemed to be coming from right up the path.

Ahead of us the path opened into a clearing where a small group of people had gathered. Someone was beating a drum. A fire flickered and the old man who had scared our pigeon was butchering the goat.

We had stumbled onto a secret Kikuyu oathing ceremony. My back felt as if a gray, hairy caterpillar was crawling down it. The old man we'd seen really was a Kikuyu mundu mugo, or what we would call a witch doctor. My dad had told me about the custom of oathing, which had bound the Kikuyu people in making promises or covenants in their traditional culture. Then it had been the binding force during the Mau Mau fight for independence when the Kikuyu freedom fighters administered the blood oath, which forced people to promise to support the fight against colonialism. They also had to promise not to betray the freedom fighters who hid in the forests to battle against the British army.

That was years before. Kenya had since won its independence, but my dad had said the oathing was being revived for political reasons.

I crawled next to Matt. "It's an oathing ceremony," I whispered. "Let's get out of here or we'll be in trouble. It's a tribal secret."

Just then the old man whirled his head and stared right at the bush we were hiding behind. He shouted something and two young men walked toward us. Matt stood up and yelled, "Run!" We ran.

Dodging small trees, I managed to get back to the path first. But despite my fear, I couldn't run away without knowing what had happened to the others. I stopped and Jon sped by. Dave passed me next, his long legs hurtling him along. Then Matt stumbled into the path and together we started running.

We didn't stop until we reached our tree fort. Our pursuers hadn't chased us very far. I guess they'd just wanted to scare us off.

In the safety of our tree house, with the rope ladder pulled up, we discussed what we'd seen. I explained what I knew about the oathing ceremony. The others listened closely.

Then Matt asked, "Do Christians take this oath?"

"No," I answered. "The oath involves swearing by the traditional gods and spirits of the ancestors. My dad says a lot of Christians have been persecuted for refusing to take the oath."

"That's strange," said Matt, shaking his head. "Did you see that one well-dressed man in the group of oath-takers?"

"Yeah," I answered, "what about him?"

"Well," Matt said, "he looked a lot like one of the church leaders for this area. I went with my dad a few weeks ago to a seminar and one of the preachers looked just like that man. At least I think so."

We were all puzzled by our experience. But we agreed not to tell our parents. We thought they might decide not to let us go down to our tree house in the forest any more.

We headed home in the cool of the approaching night. We saw two pigeons but didn't even try to pot one. That's how much the experience had upset us.

CHAPTER TWO

Safari Rally

By the next week we had almost forgotten the oathing incident. Excitement ran high. This was the day Matt's dad had promised to take the four of us to watch the Safari Rally. Each year this four-day car race attracted cars and drivers from all over the world. The drivers would race their cars at top speeds over some of the roughest roads in Africa. This was the first day of the race, and the cars would pass within ten miles of Rugendo.

We gathered at Matt's house at about ten in the morning. We each had a packed lunch. Matt's mom sent along a vacuum jug of iced tea. In addition to our food, we each had scorecards and a printed program telling the names of all the drivers, their numbers, and what kind of car they drove. Matt had his radio turned on but we couldn't hear much more than the roar of engines as the cars were flagged off the starting ramp at two-minute intervals from Kenyatta Conference Center in Nairobi. In an hour they would be driving by Rugendo.

Matt's dad came out. We all jumped into the Land Rover and he backed it out the driveway. Soon we were bumping down the road.

Matt's dad leaned back and told us he'd found a good place to watch the cars. "I saw it last week when I was doing a leadership seminar at one of the churches. There's a hairpin curve with a giant hole in the middle. It rained this week so I think there'll be water in the hole. That should make the curve slick with mud. There's a place where we can park the Land Rover away from the road. Then we can climb above the curve and watch the cars. They'll have to go slowly or they'll knock the bottoms off of their cars and skid off the road. We'll have a great view."

"Sounds neat," we all enthused from the back. Matt grinned. I could tell he was proud of his dad.

"Wow, this is perfect," Jon shouted as we arrived at the spot. He scrambled up the hill.

We followed, and soon had gathered at the top like a troop of baboons. We huddled around the radio, trying to hear the reports from Nairobi. But the steep mountains in the area made the reception fuzzy.

I heard the car first. "Here comes one!" I said. "Can you hear it?" Matt turned off the radio and we all listened. Sure enough, a throaty roar began to build to a crescendo. Then a car burst into view.

"It's Bjorkman, the Swedish driver," said Dave, our detail man. He had spotted the number **3** on the door of the car and had looked in his program. "He started third but he's already passed two cars. He must really be sailing. He'll bust his car long before the finish."

We all watched, transfixed, as Bjorkman went into a controlled skid around a bend in the road. Then he approached the hairpin curve beneath us. He hit the water hole at full speed. Water splashed into the air. Then the car started sliding on the glassy-slick mud.

"He's out of control," Matt murmured hoarsely. It seemed to happen in slow motion. The car looked like it was floating off the road. Then we heard the harsh sound of branches breaking as the car dipped into the ravine.

As we watched, too astonished to move, we saw both drivers emerge from where the car had stopped, tilted at a steep angle like a sinking boat.

"Come on, boys," Matt's dad said "Let's see if we can help."

Just then another rally car roared by. This one, driven by a local driver, slowed down at the curve and then accelerated up the hill, spraying mud behind it.

Staying well off the road, we ran down to see if we could help Bjorkman. Bjorkman's co-driver, dressed in white coveralls, pulled himself out from under the front of the car.

"Anything broken?" Matt's dad asked.

"It looks okay," the co-driver answered. "Just some bent bodywork. We were lucky not to hit any big trees. But we're really stuck in here and I don't know how we'll get the car out."

The two Swedes shook their heads. "We're out of the race now," Bjorkman said. "And after so much practice and so much money to get here. What a waste."

"Don't give up yet," Matt's dad said. "If you want to finish the race, I can get you out."

Bjorkman laughed. "So could I if my service crew were here and we had a strong vehicle with a winch. But my work crew is scheduled to meet us several hours down the road. By the time they get here and pull me out we'd be time-barred at the next control point."

"I have a Land Rover parked just up the hill," Matt's dad said. "And I have a winch. I've pulled cars out of worse situations than this. My guess is we'll have you back on the road in less than fifteen minutes. Will that keep you in the race?"

Bjorkman gave Matt's dad an incredulous look. "You have a Land Rover here? Go get it! I've already gained ten minutes. We'd only be five minutes behind."

We ran up the hill to get the Land Rover. Another rally car roared by, flicking mud and stones in our direction. We hardly noticed it. We were actually helping a rally driver. What a story this would be to tell the other kids when school started again in a month.

Bjorkman and his co-driver had taken a shovel and dug out the area behind the car's wheels. Matt's dad parked carefully so he wouldn't obstruct any other rally cars driving past. Then he hopped out and quickly attached the steel winch cable to the car. Slowly and steadily he pulled the car out until it bumped over the ridge and stood back on all four wheels on the road.

Bjorkman made a quick check of the suspension, then jumped in and started the engine, which roared to life. The car's hood vibrated wildly on top of the pulsating engine. Bjorkman looked out and asked, "How can I thank you for all your help?"

Matt's dad smiled. "There's no need to thank us. We're Christians and we follow what Jesus taught when he told us to help our neighbors in any way we can."

"Well," Bjorkman said reaching out his hand, "I do thank you. Very much." Matt's dad gripped his hand firmly and shook it. "And thank you boys, too," Bjorkman said waving to us.

Then, determined to make up for lost time, Bjorkman released the clutch and raced up the hill, fishtailing in the mud.

"Boy, that was exciting!" Matt exclaimed. "Did you see inside the car? They had a roll bar and a tachometer and all kinds of fancy equipment. Both drivers had helmets with earphones, so they could talk to each other while they're driving."

"Yeah, that was great," Dave agreed. "The inside of that car looked like the cockpit of an airplane, it had so many instruments." He started to identify all the things he'd seen using technical names.

None of the rest of us understood him but we respected his knowledge.

"Can you believe he slid off the road right in front of us so we'd have the chance to help him?" I asked, still awed by what had happened.

More cars passed, but we weren't as excited anymore just watching them pass. We kept remembering what it was like actually talking to a driver, looking inside his car, and helping him.

"I think the Lord had him slide off the road right where he did so we could help him and be an example of the love of Jesus," Matt's dad said. The missionaries at Rugendo were always saying things like that. But this time we understood what he meant. We all felt pretty good when the last car whizzed past and we clambered back into the Land Rover for the trip home.

On the way home, Jon said something that got us going on a new project. "I'd really like to be a rally driver. Wouldn't that be fun! Driving fast along these roads, doing controlled skids around the corners and stuff."

We all agreed. Then Matt said, "We're not old enough to drive cars, but what if we had a bicycle safari? We could set up a route around Rugendo with a starting ramp, control points, and a finish line. Our parents could help us with the timing, and we could have a race."

Like I said, Matt always comes up with ideas. That's why we made him our club captain.

"A bike race!" I said excitedly. "That would be great." The others began talking about the bike race. Jon told us how he'd skid around corners. Dave methodically described how he'd build a starting ramp.

When we got home that afternoon we were tired and muddy. But we had a story to tell our families about helping the Swedish drivers.

We could hardly wait for the next day, when Matt had scheduled a meeting at our tree house to plan the bike safari.

CHAPTER THREE

Planning the Bike Safari

I arrived first at our tree house the next day. As the secretary, I had remembered to stuff a folded piece of paper and a pencil into my jeans pocket for taking notes of the meeting.

I climbed the tree to where we had hidden our rope ladder in a hole. I pulled the ladder out and secured it to a large branch. Then I climbed into the tree house and pulled the ladder in after me.

I smoothed my paper out on the rough board that served as my note-taking desk. The point of my pencil had broken off while I was running through the forest, so I dug into my pocket for my Swiss army knife and whittled my pencil to a sharp point. Then I heard someone calling from below.

"Who goes there?" I yelled.

"It's me, Jon," answered the voice below.

"Give the secret pass code," I instructed him.

"Rugendo Rhinos really rally behind rare rhinos," Jon said rapidly.

I threw down the ladder. I knew it was Jon all the time but Matt always insisted we never let anyone up who didn't repeat the pass code.

Pretty soon Dave and Matt showed up and we started the meeting.

"The meeting will come to order," Matt announced. "We'll skip roll call today because we know we're all here. Now, our first and only item of business today is to organize this bike race. Agreed?"

We all agreed.

"First," Matt continued, "who gets to enter?"

"We do, of course," answered Jon.

"I know that," Matt answered. "But if we're the only ones who enter, we won't have much competition. I was thinking we could open the race up to any kid, black or white, as long as they have a bike to ride."

"Great idea," I said, making a note that the rally would be open to anyone with a bike.

"I think we should have an entry fee as well," Matt went on. "Of course, none of us would have to pay because we're organizing the race. But for the others, we should make them pay a fee, just like in the Safari Rally."

"Wait a minute," Dave objected. "I don't think that's really fair. I'm sure there will be some kids who will want to race who won't have money to enter. What do we need the extra money for, anyway?"

Matt scratched his head. He always did this when he was thinking. "Yeah," he said slowly, "we wouldn't want anyone left out because he couldn't pay. I'd feel like a mean old hyena if that happened. But the reason I thought we'd have an entry fee is so we could use that money to buy a trophy for the winner. I saw some neat trophies at the Nairobi Sports House the last time I went there to get the hole in my soccer ball fixed."

We all liked the idea of a trophy, but we didn't want to leave anyone out. I suggested we have a five shillings entry fee, but that we make it optional. When a person entered, we would explain to him the money would be used to buy a trophy. If a person couldn't pay, he could still enter. But the more people who paid, the better the trophy would be.

With that agreed, Dave said his dad

would help build a starting ramp and a finishing ramp just like the Safari Rally cars had in Nairobi.

"Now we're getting somewhere," Jon said enthusiastically. "Man! Real ramps!"

The meeting went on most of the morning. I said I would get my father to time the take-off so each bike rider would leave at one-minute intervals. Dave said his dad would handle the timing at the finish. Matt said he'd ask his mother to bake some cookies and have iced tea at the finish.

"Looks like all that's left is to map out the race course," I said, surveying the list of items I had written down. Right away everyone had his own idea of where the race should go.

"We should start down by the old cemetery," Jon began before Dave interrupted him, saying, "No, I say we start in front of my house because..." He never got a chance to finish his sentence.

Matt stood to his feet shouting, "Order! Order!" We quieted down in a hurry and listened to our leader. "This is what we'll do," Matt said. "This afternoon we'll meet at the soccer field on our bikes. We will then ride over every inch of road on the mission station. We will do it together. But, as you can see, the final decision can't be made by a committee." Looking at me, he asked, "Tell me, Dean, how many people map out the route for the Safari Rally?"

I knew the answer because each year I studied the souvenir program I bought for watching the Safari cars. "It's one man," I said. "He drives all over Kenya deciding which roads the cars will use. Sometimes he has a companion on his trips, but the decision is made by one man."

I felt a bit disappointed. I knew what Matt was driving at. If we tried to make the decision as a club, we'd just squabble. We'd already demonstrated that. Now Matt would decide on the route himself.

"Right," Matt said after hearing my answer. "So we'll ride the roads together. Each person can point out what he likes about certain parts of the roads. But the final decision will be made by," he paused for emphasis, "Dean."

"By *me?*" I asked, hardly believing what I'd just heard. "Why me, Matt? You're the club captain."

"Yeah, I'm the captain, but you're the guy who spends all that time studying the real Safari. I think you'd do the best job of setting up a route for our bike safari."

The meeting dismissed and we climbed down and hid the rope ladder as usual. I was thrilled by the job I'd been given.

Far away in the woods we heard the harsh, nasal cry of a blue monkey. Usually we'd have tracked it down. But today we wanted to get home for lunch so we could spend the afternoon checking out the roads we would use for the bike safari.

When I got home I took out a large sheet of paper and sketched a map of the station so I could write notes on it during the afternoon. Then in the evening I could finalize the route.

At lunch my mother scolded me for eating so fast. I told my parents about our plan for the bike safari and how we were going out after lunch to discuss the route. I also asked my dad if he could do the timing at the start of the race. He smiled and said he'd be glad to.

"That's good, because I already told the guys you would. Goodbye, Mom and Dad. I have to meet the other Rhinos at the soccer field."

"Wait just a minute, young man," Mom said. "Are you forgetting that you wash lunch dishes?"

"Oh, yeah. I did forget, Mom. Honest." I

set down my map and started running the water.

"What's this?" Dad asked, picking up the map I'd drawn.

"Oh, it's just a map of the station," I answered. "I drew it so I could make notes this afternoon. We're all going to ride around, but Matt says I get to make the final decision on the actual route for our race."

"That's great," Dad said. "I'm really proud of you, Dean." Then his eyes narrowed as he scanned the map I'd drawn.

I turned and began washing the dishes.

"This map..." Dad said slowly after he'd studied it.

I was embarrassed. "I know it's not very good."

But he stopped me. "No, it's very detailed. I like it. But there's a road I don't think you know about. It would be an ideal place for part of your bike race."

A road I didn't know about? How could it be? We Rhinos thought we'd explored every inch of Rugendo and the surrounding woods on our hunts. "Where is this road, Dad?" I asked, putting down the dish rag.

"Come over here to the table," he said. Then, spreading the map out, he pointed to a place just east of the station. "In the 1800s

Rugendo used to be a camp for Arab slave traders. Here they would gather slaves from all over this area. When they had enough, they would head for the coast. The slave caravan path grew into a fair-sized road. It's not used anymore, but it's still enough of a path for your bikes. The road goes right along here." He took his pen and drew the road onto my map.

"When the mission started here in the early 1900s, the first missionaries came in on that slave road. But then with the coming of the railroad, a new road was built to the south to link up with the nearest railroad station. Since then, all traffic has gone out on the main road over here." He pointed it out on the map and I nodded.

"But how did you know about the old slave caravan road?" I asked.

"That's another long story," Dad said with a laugh. "To make it short, an old Kikuyu man who still remembers escaping a slave raid on his village told me about it. When I was skeptical, he offered to show me the place. I went with him and saw it several years ago. It's a bit overgrown, but the base of the old slave road is very smooth and it would be excellent for riding bikes on."

I shook my head in amazement. "A real

slave caravan road. Won't the other guys be surprised! Thanks, Dad. This will make our bike safari really exciting."

I headed for the door and my bike.

"Wait a minute, Dean," Dad said.

I turned, expecting some other information on the slave road. Instead he pointed at the sink. "Dishes, remember?"

"Oh, yeah," I answered. "Dishes."

CHAPTER FOUR

Plotting the Course

"Sorry I'm late," I apologized to the others as I skidded my bike to a stop by the soccer field.

"It's about time," Matt snapped. "We've been waiting for at least ten minutes. What kept you?"

I shrugged and tried to hide my wrinkled dish-water hands. I took out the map I'd made and spread it on the ground. "Here's a map I made of the station," I said. "You can lead the way, Matt." Matt started to push off on his new ten-speed bike.

"Dave, you and Jon can make any comments you want as we ride around. I'll write all the comments down in this little notebook. Then tonight I'll put the notes on the map, decide on a final route, and draw a new map." By the end I was shouting. I'm not sure Matt heard, but Jon and Dave nodded and were already pedaling away.

Matt headed for Hospital Hill. It was a steep hill that went from the church down to the mission hospital. I secretly called it Dead Man's Hill. And not just because the old mission cemetery stood at the bottom. I clearly remembered trying to navigate the hill on my tricycle when I was only four. As the front wheel began to spin around faster and faster, my feet had been pushed off the pedals. And on that trike, back-pedaling was the only means of braking. Knowing I had little chance of reaching the bottom in one piece, I headed my little blue trike into the first culvert and had a tremendous crash, flying over the handlebars and landing in the grass. Hence the name Dead Man's Hill. Even to this day my stomach flips whenever I have to ride down that hill.

Matt braked to a stop at the top of Hospital Hill. "Get this down, Dean," he said as I pulled up. "This hill would be a great stretch for our bike safari. We can really fly down here."

I gulped and hoped no one else noticed. "I'll note that Matt. But actually I'd hoped to route the safari *up* this hill," I said trying to keep the tremble out of my voice.

"Up! Never!" Matt scoffed. "We'd all have to get off our bikes and push. Nahh! It has to be downhill." Then with a whoop he started straight down, followed by Dave and Jon.

Taking a deep breath, I followed, squeezing my brake handles tightly and praying they wouldn't be worn down to the metal. I managed to reach the bottom without making it plain to the rest how scared I was.

We kept pedaling around the station, stopping every so often to make comments. I jotted down notes. At about 5:30 we pulled up again at the soccer field, after exploring all the roads of Rugendo.

"Well, that's it," Matt said. "It's up to you now, Dean, to make the final decisions." He paused, then added, "But we'd better go down Hospital Hill, not up."

I smiled tightly. "You bet, Matt. But we're not done with our ride today. There's one more road I'd like for us to look at."

"What do you mean, one more road?" asked Dave. "We've been on every road there is! And my legs are tired enough to prove it!"

I pulled out the map and told them my dad's story about the old slave road. They all wanted to see it.

"It'll be dark in about an hour," Matt said,

"but we'll just have time to see if this old road is good enough for riding bikes. Imagine! An old slave road right here at Rugendo!"

I led the way. We passed the local primary school and then saw some old ruined buildings. "My dad said these houses were the first ones the missionaries lived in when they came here," I commented.

"We knew about these old houses," answered Matt. "We just never knew about the *slave* road."

We passed the houses and rode into a big thicket of large trees. "Right through here," I said, dodging between two pencil cedar trees. The late afternoon sun didn't penetrate into the forest and it was dark.

"Kind of spooky," Jon said. He was usually a brave adventurer, but at ten years old he was the youngest in our group, and darkness wasn't much of an adventure for him.

"It's just on the other side here, according to my dad," I said, trying to sound encouraging. I felt a bit scared myself. It was now after six, and darkness falls quickly at the equator. I recognized a large boulder my dad had described as being the entrance to the road. "There it is!" I cried, pointing.

The trees thinned out and the lingering

rays of sunshine made it easier to see. "Pretty firm," Dave remarked, getting off his bike and walking on the path. He looked almost like his dad testing a river bed before attempting to cross. "Yes," Dave approved, "we could ride pretty fast on this."

Matt loved it. "This is great! We could start the race up here at the top. Wouldn't that be something? Holding our bike safari on an old slave road?"

Seeing the other guys excited made me happy, too. This had been a good idea.

We kept riding. After about a quarter of a mile, we came to a rock slide which had covered the old trail. "Looks like this is where we'll have to start our race," I said. "We can't ride our bikes any farther back up in here."

"It'll be great," Jon said. We sat there for a few minutes, delighted with the idea of revealing the old slave road to the other kids who would enter the race.

Matt got up. "We'd better go," he said looking at his watch. "It'll be dark soon."

"Yeah, let's go," I said. "I'm glad you like this old road. I'm not sure of the whole route yet, but this will definitely be the starting section."

"And we'll ride down Hospital Hill," Matt reminded me.

"That's right, Matt," I said, hoping he didn't notice my lack of enthusiasm.

We began riding down the gentle slope. Just before the thicket of trees there was a sharp, hairpin bend that turned right and then left to avoid a deep ravine. The ravine was choked with vines, ferns, and stinging nettles. "This curve will be a thriller," Jon, who was riding beside me, said. "We'll have to see how fast we can go without losing control and skidding into the ravine. Boy, it's deep down there." He continued on, peering down into the threatening gully.

I nodded and gripped more tightly to my brakes.

We were in the middle of the thicket when the sun dropped. We could almost feel it get darker. That's how night comes in Kenya. Within five or ten minutes it would be completely dark. I had been amazed when we'd gone to the States a few years before. It took all evening for the sun to set during the summertime.

The path through the trees was narrow. "Don't worry, we're almost home," Matt assured us. The tone in his voice was not as confident as his words. I could tell he was worried. We sped through the trees.

I spotted the man first. "Look over there,"

I shouted. "Someone is watching us!"

Dave ran his bike into the back of mine as I braked and we both fell into the green undergrowth.

"Ouch!" Dave screamed. "I fell into stinging nettles. My whole leg hit the plant. It feels like I have electricity running through my leg."

I had fallen on one arm and it had brushed against a stinging nettle, too. The plants grew thick in the highland forests of Kenya. They didn't do any permanent damage, but they stung like fire if you touched one.

"What's all this about? "Matt asked, irritated. "First you tell us that someone is watching us and now you're complaining that you fell into stinging nettles."

"I really *did* see a man," I said, defending myself. "He was running along parallel to us and staring right at you, Matt."

"Why would someone stare at us?" Matt asked. "I think you just saw a shadow. Or maybe a blue monkey. Come on, let's get moving. This place gives me the creeps."

We were soon out of the woods and speeding down the road toward our homes. I knew I hadn't just seen a shadow. It was a man. And his face was familiar, but I just couldn't remember where I'd seen it before.

We got to Jon's house first. He waved and pulled into his driveway. Dave peeled off next. Matt's house was next to mine. We said goodbye as the last of the day's sunlight dropped behind the volcanic mountains to the west, leaving a ribbon of orange and red. My dad was probably taking another photograph of yet another breathtaking sunset.

I felt tired and my mind puzzled over the man I'd seen in the woods. But I decided to put it out of my mind. After supper I laid out the final route for our bike safari with the start at the rock slide on the old slave trail. I even included a section going down Hospital Hill. I made a mental note to check my brakes the next day.

I drew a detailed map and got permission from my dad to make copies the next day on the photocopy machine at his office.

Then I went to bed.

CHAPTER FIVE

A Case of Mistaken Identity?

The next day I ran off copies of the map at my dad's office before taking them over to Matt's house. We then picked up Dave and Jon and began recruiting riders for our bike safari. We went to the homes of the other missionaries on the station and got four other kids who wanted to ride. Then we faced a problem.

All the kids we'd asked were guys. Then someone's sister heard about it. Her name was Jill and she was in my class at school. She insisted we let her ride in the bike safari.

"Oh, no!" Matt told her hastily. "Boys only in this race. It's really going to be tough, and no girl could ever keep up."

"But when you asked my brother you said anyone who had a bike could enter. I have a bike and I want to enter. I don't see why I can't. Anyway, I'm a faster rider than my brother," Jill said, crossing her arms and glaring at us.

"Uh, give us a chance to talk about this, okay, Jill?" Matt said. "We'll let you know later."

Jill looked at her watch. "Okay. I'll give you one hour to decide. And if you don't let me, I'm telling my parents you guys have been bullying me."

"Whew! What do we do now?" Matt asked as Jill walked away.

Jon knew what we should do. "Tell her she can't race. We're the organizers and we say boys only."

"But we said anyone with a bike," Matt said, "and we can't go back on that or make up new rules now. How stupid of me! I never thought girls would want to race in our bike safari or I'd have made the rule say any boy with a bike could ride."

I agreed with Matt that we couldn't go back on the rule we'd made. I didn't see any reason why Jill shouldn't be allowed to ride in the race, but I couldn't say that openly or the other Rhinos would accuse me of liking a girl.

We sat silently for a while. Then I had an idea. "We're sort of copying the Safari Rally with our bike race, aren't we?" I asked slowly.

Everyone agreed.

"Well, sometimes ladies drive in the Safari Rally," I said. "In fact, in 1963, when terrible floods allowed only seven cars to finish the race, one of the seven finishing cars was driven by two ladies. So if the Safari Rally has women drivers, we could, too. I mean, if you all agree."

Matt nodded his head. He looked at Dave and Jon. "What do you say?"

Dave grudgingly said it was okay with him as long as I was sure ladies drove in the real Safari. I assured him it was true and offered to show him the story of The Magnificent Seven of 1963 in my official history book about the Safari Rally.

Jon agreed, too. "Okay," he said, "let her race. But let's beat her so badly she won't ever want to race against boys again."

We went to Jill's house and told her we'd decided she could enter. She was thrilled. She even paid double the entry fee when she heard it would be spent on a trophy for the winner.

At the end of the day we had ten riders entered in the Rugendo Rhinos Bicycle Safari. There were the four of us, four other guys from the mission station, Jill, and Benjamin, the Kikuyu pastor's son. Everyone had a copy of the map and we gave them three days to practice riding the course which covered a distance of almost three miles. Since this was our school vacation, we set the race for the following Tuesday morning at ten.

In the meantime, we Rhinos were busy helping build the ramps with Dave's dad. We also had to recruit parents to man checkpoints at designated spots on the route so no one could cheat by taking a short cut. Matt also had to go to Nairobi with his dad to buy a trophy for the winner. He found a neat one at Nairobi Sports House, with a gold-colored bicycle rider mounted on a wooden stand.

The Sunday before the race, we all attended the Rugendo church as usual. I always had to sit with my parents. Matt, Dave, and Jon sat by themselves in a different row from their families. Sometimes I envied them. But my mom always said we should sit together as a family.

I looked up at the pulpit. Benjamin's dad, Pastor Kariuki, introduced a guest speaker from a nearby district. With a smile, Pastor Kariuki said the speaker was not only a good friend and brother in the Lord, but also his cousin.

After the introduction, the speaker stood

up. I almost jumped out of my seat when I saw him. I sat straight up, straining to get a good view of the man. I couldn't believe it! He looked exactly like the well-dressed man we'd seen at the oathing ceremony. Matt had said the man at the oathing ceremony resembled a church leader his father had taught. But could this really be the same man? Maybe I'd made a mistake in identifying him.

I didn't hear much of the sermon, even though it was translated into English from Kikuyu for our benefit. My mind went back to the clearing where I'd seen the old mundu mugo (witch doctor) oathing people. The picture came back like replaying a video tape. *This man had been at the oathing ceremony.*

I had a feeling I'd seen him somewhere else, too. Maybe preaching at the church last year? I didn't know. The image of his face at the oathing ceremony made it impossible for me to concentrate on where else I may have seen him.

After church we went home. While my mom finished putting dinner together, I asked my dad about the man who had preached.

"Dad," I began, "do you know the guy who preached today?"

"You mean Reverend Kimani? Yes, I know him," Dad answered. "He's one of the strongest Kikuyu church leaders in the area. Why do you want to know?"

"Well, it's just that I think we saw him a week or so ago while we were hunting pigeons," I said. "And we saw him taking the oath in a secret ceremony led by a Kikuyu witch doctor."

"What are you talking about?" Dad asked.

I explained to him how we'd been hunting and had stumbled onto the ceremony. "And one of the men standing there taking the oath was the man who preached in church today," I finished.

My dad frowned. "I hadn't realized they were oathing so close to Rugendo," he said. "This oathing business is really serious, Dean. You and your friends had better stay closer to home on your hunts. No telling what would have happened to you if you'd been caught down there. I really don't think anyone would hurt you, but these oaths of loyalty to the tribe and clan are very strong. People who've taken the oath will do exactly as they're told. During Kenya's freedom war, called the Mau Mau Uprising by the colonial government, these oaths bound Kikuyu people to fight for freedom and even to kill white settlers."

"But why was Reverend Kimani taking that oath if he is a Christian?" I asked. "You told me Christians were resisting the oath and even being persecuted for their stand against oathing."

My dad laughed gently. "I'm convinced you saw an oathing ceremony in the woods," he said. "But I'm also convinced you did not see Reverend Kimani. Like you said, the Christians have been resisting the oath taking. And one of the most vocal leaders encouraging Christians to resist the oath is Reverend Kimani. He even wrote an article for our magazine, urging Christians to stand firm against this oathing business."

"But we *saw* him," I said. "And he took the oath."

"Dean, I think you saw a man who may have looked like him, but you didn't see Reverend Kimani," Dad answered. "You know how so many Kikuyu people look similar to us. It's kind of funny. The other day I was talking to an old Kikuyu man. I introduced him to some of the other missionaries at the office. Then he said he couldn't tell missionaries apart because all white people look the same to him!" Dad laughed at his story.

I laughed with him. I saw his point, but I'd been so sure.

"So you think it's just a case of mistaken identity?" I asked. "That really wasn't Reverend Kimani we saw at the oathing ceremony, but someone who looked like him?"

Dad put an arm on my shoulder. "Yes, just a case of mistaken identity, Dean."

Mom called us to dinner and we sat down to a warthog roast with all the trimmings. What a meal! The meat was tender and juicy. Dad had shot the warthog on a hunting trip the month before, and we'd stocked our freezer with meat. It tasted so good it made me forget my suspicions about Reverend Kimani and the oath-taking ceremony we Rhinos had seen.

CHAPTER SIX

The Race

I woke shortly before six A.M. I could hear the birds singing in the bottlebrush tree outside my window. I jumped out of bed and started to get dressed. This was the day of the bike safari. All the preparations had been made. The race would start at ten sharp. Only four hours from now! I had been practicing riding my bike over the route for the past few days. I knew I had a good chance of winning, as I was one of the biggest guys entered in the race and could beat anyone going up hill. I still wouldn't admit to my fellow Rhinos that I was afraid to go downhill. I had worn my brakes down almost to the metal. Matt would be my main competition because he loved flying downhill. His brakes still had the rubber nubs on them as if they'd never been used. Before going downstairs, I asked God to help me overcome my fear of going downhill.

In the kitchen I poured myself a bowl of cereal and made some toast. My dad came in to fix coffee. "Up pretty early, aren't you?" he asked.

"Today's the bike safari, Dad," I answered.

He smiled. "I know, I'm the timer, remember? But I would have thought you could have used some extra rest. After all, the race doesn't start until ten."

I shrugged. "I couldn't sleep. Anyway, I have to help set up the starting ramp."

Dad put his hand on my shoulder. "You're excited and that's good. Save up some of that energy for the race and you'll win for sure."

After breakfast I went over to Matt's house. I threw a rock at his window. No answer. I threw a handful of rocks. Matt's window opened. "What is it?" he asked, still half-asleep.

"Safari day," I said. "We have to get the ramp set up and make sure all the parents know where to go."

"What time is it?" Matt muttered, looking at his watch. "Not even seven. Dean, you're a fanatic!"

But he got up and in a few minutes he

opened the door. I sat at the table while he had some eggs for breakfast. His mom asked us which checkpoint she was supposed to run. We tried to explain it to her but she got mixed up. So after breakfast we had her drive the car to where she was to stand and explained again what she was supposed to do.

By now both Jon and Dave had joined us. We made sure all the other parents knew where to be and what to do. We thought we'd made it clear before, but if Matt's mom was any indication, we thought we'd better be sure.

Then we went to Dave's house. The finishing ramp was already set up in their driveway. His dad had the starting ramp all ready to go in the back of his pickup truck. We put our bikes in the truck and drove as near to the starting point on the old slave trail as we could get.

We carried the ramp the rest of the way and set it up. Then we waited for the other riders to arrive. I had thought to bring my canteen along. It might slow me up a little bit, but I knew the water would taste good at the checkpoints. I pulled out the canteen and took a swig, wiped the neck, and passed it around to the others.

At about 9:30 most of the riders had come and we had a draw to see who would start. We divided the draw up so the younger kids would lead off. Of the older kids, I drew the last number. Matt started just before me.

My dad had arrived with his stop watch and at precisely ten A.M. the first rider rolled down the ramp and pedaled furiously down the trail. Every minute, another took off. Finally only Matt and I were left.

"This is it, Dean," Matt said to me. "Good luck." With that he pushed his bike onto the ramp. His eyes narrowed to slits as my dad gave the final countdown. Then he flew down the ramp. I shook my head. I would be lucky if I could catch up with him. But I knew I had to try. That's one thing my parents had taught me: Keep trying right up to the end.

At last it was my turn. Just before I pushed off I caught a glimpse of Matt's back far ahead right before the sharp turn around the ravine. I pedaled hard to catch up. At the ravine corner I did a controlled skid, expecting to see Matt near the bottom of the long hill that led back to the station. But I couldn't see him anywhere. Puzzled, I assumed he had taken off at laser speed.

The hill after the ravine was so steep I felt

as if I was driving down a cliff. My hands began to grip my brakes. *No! I have to ride down this hill flat out or I'll never catch Matt,* I told myself. *That's why I can't see him. He's gone down the hill at full speed.*

Breathing a prayer to the Lord to keep me safe I released my grip on the brakes and kept pedaling. My bike went faster and faster, but this time I was determined not to slow down. Maybe I shouldn't have been so determined. At the bottom of the hill the road turned sharply to the right. I rode into the curve too fast and my bike slid sideways underneath me. My bike fell and dirt and rocks tore chunks of skin from my leg. Choking back tears, I remounted and pushed off again. *Only a few seconds lost in my fall and I'm sure I've gained time on Matt,* I told myself. I'd never gone down a hill so fast in my life. I felt great. I thanked the Lord for answering my prayer.

Soon I saw a rider. But it wasn't Matt. I passed, giving the thumbs up sign as I sped by. I could see some other riders ahead. But not Matt. *This is really strange,* I thought. I wondered if he had somehow put a motorcycle engine on his bike. I laughed at the thought, and began pushing myself even harder and passed a few more riders.

I wrote my name in at each checkpoint, but I was in such a hurry, I forgot to look for Matt's name. I knew he was ahead of me and I wanted to catch him. But I never did. I came up the final hill and I could hear people cheering. Some others had already finished the race, but the winner would be the one who had completed the course in the fastest time based on his starting time. Since I had started last, my time had to be better than all those I'd passed. And the timer shouted out that my time was the best of those who had finished. I had won the Rugendo Rhinos Bicycle Safari! I felt great. I must have beaten Matt's time by just a few seconds.

"Where's Matt?" I asked after the joy of winning had settled in.

"He's not in yet," said Jon. "You must have really been flying to pass him. You know what a dare devil rider he is!"

"Not in? Are you sure, Jon?" I asked. "He started in front of me and I never passed him. I chased him the whole race. That's why I rode so fast. How can he not be in?"

But Jon was sure. We checked with Dave's dad who had timed the finish. He confirmed that Matt hadn't come in. Then where was he?

We began asking the other riders. No one had seen Matt pass them during the race. By now all the riders had finished the race. Except Matt. We began to get worried. We forgot the presentation of the trophy and the iced tea and cookies. Something had happened to Matt.

We told our parents about our concern. Matt had not signed in at any of the checkpoints! Soon everyone gathered around trying to decide what to do.

I said the last place I'd seen Matt was going into the ravine corner on the old slave road.

"That's the best place to start looking," said my dad. "There's a steep drop-off there. Maybe Matt went over the edge."

"Knowing the way Matt rides his bike, I wouldn't be surprised," Matt's dad said grimly. "But before we search, let's pray."

After praying we jumped into Matt's dad's Land Rover to look for Matt.

CHAPTER SEVEN

Searching for Matt

When we reached the corner by the ravine we jumped out and began searching. "Matt, Matt," we called. But the trees and leaves in the forest swallowed the sound and our only answer was an eerie silence.

We looked around the edge of the ravine. Jon, with his excellent tracking abilities, discovered the first clue. "Over here!" he called. "The grass has been trampled and there are crushed leaves on these bushes. This must be where he went down."

We hurried to Jon and, peering down into the thick growth in the ravine, we called for Matt again. But once more we received no answer.

Matt's dad shook his head. "I can't figure it out. If Matt had skidded into the ravine, he should have fallen in over there, where his speed would have been the greatest. But if he'd made it around the curve, his speed here would have been rather slow. It just doesn't make sense."

We began climbing down the steep side of the ravine, trying to avoid the nettles. I had shorts on and soon my legs felt like they had an electric current surging down the skin from the powerful stings. But I kept on, desperately searching for Matt.

Jon led the way with the grownups. They knew he had a knack for following a trail and they used his skills wisely.

Halfway down the slope he stopped and pointed to something. We gathered around. "His bike was here all right," he said pointing out the tracks of Matt's bike tires. "But he must have carried it from here, because there are no more bike tracks after this. There are footprints. But they go further down the ravine."

I couldn't figure out what was going on. If Matt had fallen into the ravine, and if he'd had any strength left, he would have pushed the bike back up the hill. Or at least have crawled up the hill and called for help. But to carry his bike and go deeper into the ravine? It didn't make sense to me.

I felt helpless and in my heart I cried out to God to help us find Matt.

Everyone stopped again. We had come to a rocky section where a river had once flowed. Jon had lost the trail. There were no more tracks. At this point the narrow ravine we'd been following began to flatten out. There were several directions in which we could search.

My dad and Matt's dad decided to pray again. They asked God to show them the right direction to go. After praying, I had an idea. "Maybe one of us can climb a tree and try to see which way to go. I saw it work once in a movie." People looked at me strangely. I shrugged. "Well, I thought it was at least worth a try," I said.

Jon believed in me. He was already scrambling up a Cape chestnut tree. It had very few branches at the bottom, but Jon could shinny up a tree like a monkey. Near the top he stopped climbing and looked around the area. Then he slid down the tree.

"That was a good idea, Dean," he said, pointing. "I saw a small spring in that direction and I think I saw footprints in the mud."

The grownups decided it was as good a direction as any, so off we went.

Arriving at the spring, we did find

footprints. And bike tracks. But something was very wrong. This time Dave noticed it first. "There's two sets of footprints here," he said. "And these other footprints look like they belong to a grown man." It seemed that Matt and whoever was with him had stopped for a drink. And then they had left, leaving no tracks on the rocks. This time there were no tall trees to climb. We had reached the end of the trail.

In frustration I picked up a rock and hurled it into the bushes. To my surprise, I heard the clink of rock on metal. At first I thought my rock must have hit another rock. I decided to investigate.

"Come back, Dean," my father called as I began to run toward the bushes. "We have to stay together as a group. One lost boy is enough."

"But, Dad," I protested, "I threw a rock in there and it hit something metal, I'm sure of it. I just want to see what it is."

He joined me and we hurried over to the bush. We pulled up the branches and there lay Matt's bike. It wasn't damaged at all, so it didn't look like he'd crashed into the ravine.

My dad called the others over. "We've found Matt's bike," he said.

I noticed a ragged scrap of paper impaled

on the brake handle. "What's this?" I asked, pulling it off the bike. I read it, but couldn't believe my eyes. I quickly handed it to my dad and said, "It can't be true, Dad. It looks like a ransom note, but Matt can't have been kidnapped. That just can't have happened." I was forced to stop talking as I began to sob.

My dad read the note to the others: *I have the boy. If you want to see him again, leave 10,000 shillings in this very spot.*

My dad put his arm around Matt's dad. "It looks bad," my dad said, "but we know the Lord is in control." Matt's dad nodded, but I could see he was crying.

We decided we had to tell the police. But we didn't want to lose the trail while it was hot. So my dad went back to the station with the younger kids to call the police and get more help. I persuaded my dad to let Dave, Jon, and me stay on and search. Reluctantly he agreed, but he made us promise to stay close to Matt's dad. We promised.

We searched through lunch and well into the afternoon. We didn't even stop to eat. But we found nothing. At about four, my dad arrived with the Kenyan police and a few more missionaries. We searched until dark. But try as we might, we found no sign of Matt or his kidnapper.

It was as if the kidnapper had allowed us to find Matt's bike and then vanished, taking Matt with him.

We went home discouraged and very tired. What had begun as an exciting day for a bike race ended in a nightmare.

That evening after supper, everyone on the mission station gathered together and we prayed long and hard for Matt's safe return. We even called the other mission stations on the radio and they all promised to pray as well.

When we left the prayer meeting, I knew we would find Matt. I didn't know how. Things looked hopeless. But while we prayed I was reminded of how great and strong God is and how he'd answered so many prayers before. I knew he wouldn't fail us now.

CHAPTER EIGHT

The Mau Mau Cave

The next day police came with dogs and they yelped up a storm and crashed through a lot of bushes. But by the end of the day they hadn't uncovered anything new.

The police officer in charge asked some of the missionaries if they would pay the ransom money since they had no idea what else to do. Matt's dad wanted to, of course. But the mission had a policy against paying ransoms on the grounds that it would lead to more kidnappings.

Finally the police left with their apologies for not solving the case. They promised to leave some plain-clothes policemen working on it. But they called off the search parties. Whoever snatched Matt had disappeared without a clue.

"Come on," I called to Jon and Dave. "Tomorrow morning we'll meet early and go to the clubhouse. We have to figure out some way to help Matt. We need to pray and ask God to help us come up with a plan." With Matt gone, I was acting as the Rhinos' leader.

Hiking through the forest to our tree house in the early morning had a calming effect on all of us.

Once in our club house, I called our meeting together and asked Dave to pray.

"Now," I said, after the prayer, "we need to decide what we can do to help Matt. The police have given up. Our parents don't know what to do either. We're Matt's closest friends. I think it's up to us to do something."

We sat silently, trying to think of what we could do. "I know," said Jon suddenly. "We could get a hot-air balloon and then go over the whole area looking down until we find him! It would be kind of like those deluxe safaris they arrange for tourists to see animals."

We thought about that suggestion. Dave, practical as usual, finally said, "It's a good idea, Jon. But I don't think it will work. First, we don't have a hot-air balloon. And second, whoever kidnapped Matt would have him hidden somewhere and he'd probably be even harder to spot from the air. What we need to do is think of a place someone may use as a hiding place."

"The old Mau Mau cave!" I said as soon as Dave talked about a good hiding place.

"Good idea," agreed Jon, and he was halfway down the ladder. Dave and I hurried to catch up. We loped through the forest in our unique Rhino half-jog that Matt had invented. Matt had explained that it helped us go the fastest while using the least energy.

The Mau Mau cave was a natural fault in a ravine fairly close to Rugendo. My dad told me it was unlikely it had ever been used by the Mau Mau as a hideout during Kenya's struggle for independence. However, ever since we'd known about the cave, we'd called it the Mau Mau cave.

We arrived at the cave after about half an hour. "Sskss!" I hissed at Jon, using the African way of getting someone's attention. He stopped. "We have to plan how we'll do this," I whispered. "We can't just run in. If people are there they'll escape."

Dave suggested he go above the cave and come down near the east side of the entrance. Jon could wait by the west side. And I would hide in the bushes ready to catch anyone they might flush out.

Hearts thudding, we began to carry out our plan. I hunched down behind a leleshwa bush, ready to explode out and tackle anyone who might try to escape. Jon and Dave arrived at opposite sides of the entrance, signaled to each other, and began to enter the cave.

Jon and Dave hesitated for a moment, allowing their eyes to adjust to the gloom. Then they began moving silently into the cave. Within seconds I couldn't see them, only their footprints in the dust remained.

Suddenly Jon's voice called out, "We hear you. Come out of there and bring our friend Matt with you."

I crouched, ready.

I could see bodies moving in the darkness of the cave. "He's throwing things at me," shouted Dave, "and he barely missed me." A few seconds later Dave and Jon tumbled out of the cave into the dust.

"Watch out, Dean," yelled Jon. "He's coming."

I leaped from my hiding place and ran to the entrance of the cave. I met a whirling cloud of bats. They divided around us, using their sonar to see exactly where we were. They whirred the air around our heads but they didn't hit us.

"Bats!" I said, sitting down and laughing. "Is that all you found in there? Bats?"

Jon looked up sheepishly at the small black bats which were slowly returning to the cave. "I thought someone was in there," he said. "But I guess it was the the bats squeaking. I should have known, but I was sure we'd find Matt and his captor."

"Me, too," said Dave, grinning. "And when that first bat made a pass by my ear, I thought someone was throwing rocks or shooting poisoned arrows. I just started to run."

"Bats!" I said as we began dusting off. "Well, at least we know Matt isn't here. Let's go back to the clubhouse and work on a better plan."

CHAPTER NINE

Setting the Trap

We got back to the club house about mid-morning and were all thirsty. "Let's drink chai while we think," I said, and both Dave and Jon agreed. I climbed up the tree and tossed some matches down to Jon. Dave was already collecting firewood. I gathered some tea, an old black-bottomed tin pot, some dried milk, sugar, and battered enamel mugs and climbed back down.

While Jon and Dave got the fire going, I filled the pot with water from a nearby stream. Small black tadpoles swam in the water I'd fetched. I fished them out and threw them back into the stream.

Back at the fire we shook tea leaves, dried milk, and sugar into the water and boiled the mixture, stirring it occasionally with a stick that Jon cut from a wild olive tree.

When the chai was ready, we poured it into our mugs and drank it with noisy sucking noises. We'd all learned how to do this on visits to Kikuyu homes near Rugendo. It was a good way to keep your tongue from getting burned, since sucking over the hot tea before it entered your mouth cooled off the boiling-hot drink.

We finished the chai and put out the fire, then climbed up to the tree house for more privacy as we talked.

I had an idea. "Listen," I said. "The last real clue we have about Matt's kidnapping is the bush where his bike was hidden with the ransom note, right?"

"Right," said Dave.

"Well," I said slowly, "instead of trying to find Matt out there somewhere, why don't we go back to that spot. The kidnapper did ask for a ransom. Maybe he'll come back to that bush looking for the ransom money. He doesn't know our parents agreed not to leave any money."

Jon said excitedly, "We can do better than that. We can put some money in an envelope. When the kidnapper comes he'll be distracted while he checks out the envelope and we can catch him."

"Good idea," I said. I fished a key from my pocket and opened our treasury. We only had ten shillings left in the old box we used to hide our money. "It'll have to do," I said. "After all, we're not really paying a ransom, just trying to bait a trap."

We wrapped the ten shillings in an old envelope and wrote RANSOM MONEY in big letters. Then we climbed down the tree and did the Rhino half-jog back to Rugendo. We agreed to meet after lunch and go to the bush where Matt's bike had been found.

On arriving there early in the afternoon, Jon looked around and found some low trees, thick with leaves. "We'll have a perfect lookout if we hide in these trees," he said. So we put the money under the bush, climbed the trees, and waited.

We continued to wait. After an hour, I whispered to Jon and Dave, "I'm thirsty; did you guys bring anything to drink?" No one had. So we all waited, hot and thirsty. Nothing happened. My leg muscles started to cramp. I tried to find another, more comfortable position. But in doing so, I broke a small branch. It snapped with a loud crack.

Jon looked at me angrily and hissed, "If anyone was coming, he'd have left by now with all the noise you're making." We were all irritable. Hiking is fun. Waiting is agony, especially when you're balanced on a branch in a tree.

It was now about 4:30. "Let's give it up," I said to the other two. "It was a nice idea, but I guess it didn't work." Dave and I started to clamber down from the trees. Suddenly Jon waved frantically and pointed.

We looked and saw someone crouched behind a rock near the bush. It looked like a young Kenyan boy, but maybe he'd been sent as a messenger. The boy darted to the bush, seized the money, and began to run away.

"After him!" I shouted as I slid the rest of the way down the tree. All three of us were fast runners, but the Kenyan boy must have been related to one of the Kenyan runners who ran in the Olympics. He left us behind. But he ran straight for Rugendo. And, though we couldn't keep up with him, we could watch his progress as we left the forest. He ran through some cornfields, but the corn was only a few feet high so we could see where he went.

He arrived at a small wooden house near the mission hospital and he entered it. We stopped and looked at each other. The house belonged to a Kenyan man who worked in the hospital as the lab technician. Could he know what had happened? Now we had a real clue, the first since Matt had disappeared.

"Our plan worked, you guys," I said, excitedly. "But I think at this stage we need to get our parents and tell them what we've found out."

We ran to my house and explained everything to my dad. He called Matt's dad and we all went to the house by the hospital. When we got there, the lab technician greeted us warmly. Matt's dad told him what had happened. The man's eyes narrowed and he called loudly for his son. The young boy we had chased came slowly into the room.

"That's him," Jon said. "He went to the bush where we found Matt's bike and collected an envelope we had placed there hoping to lure the kidnapper. He must know something about it. He must be a messenger."

The lab technician questioned his son who answered him and then went out and brought back the envelope, with the ten shillings still inside.

He looked at our dads and said, "My son had heard about the ransom note. He thought if he waited, he might get some free money. He's been checking that bush every day since your son was kidnapped. Today he found this envelope and came here with it. I have scolded him for his greediness. But, I tell you the truth, he knows nothing about the kidnapper or about Matt. I'm sorry." He handed back the envelope with our ten shillings.

Our dads thanked him and apologized for scaring the boy. Then we all prayed together before walking slowly home.

"Well," I said to my dad, "we tried. But I guess our plan wasn't so hot."

He put his hand on my shoulder and consoled me. "It was a good plan. I'm just sorry it didn't work out. We're all as worried about Matt as you are. And it's good to see you boys trying your best to help your friend. We'll find him. I'm sure of it."

CHAPTER TEN

Mr. Kimani

The next day Dave, Jon, and I decided to ride bikes. We had no more ideas on how to help Matt. Our two ideas hadn't been exactly successful. So we decided to work off our frustration by riding bikes. It had rained the night before so the road was slightly muddy. This made the riding better, as we skidded around corners and splashed through the brown mud puddles that were scattered on the road like haphazardly thrown rugs.

By mid-morning, we decided it was time for a break. So we rode our bikes across Rugendo to the dukas (shops). We pulled up outside of the chai house and went in and, sitting at a wobbly table, ordered some chai and mandazi (mandazi are like square doughnuts without the hole).

The young man who took our order returned with the chai. The mandazi came a few minutes later, wrapped in old newspaper. Oil oozed from the newspaper and onto the plate. We had carefully watched an old man in the corner as he poured his chai out of his cup onto the saucer before drinking it. We tried it, too, and found it did an even better job of cooling down the tea than loud sucking. But now that our mandazi had arrived, we ripped pieces off and dunked them into our chai before eating them.

I had a piece of mandazi soaking in my chai when I heard someone outside say in a loud voice, "Wi mwega, are you well, Bwana Kimani?" Now, Kimani is a common name, but on this day the name jolted my memory. Reverend Kimani who had spoken in church! The one I thought we'd seen at the oathing ceremony! The one who had stared right at Matt! And, come to think of it, maybe even the same face I'd seen in the forest when we were setting up the bike safari route on the old slave trail!

"Ouch!" I said, pulling my hand out of my chai and dropping the mandazi in. "I burned myself." I then stood up and stepped outside to see which Kimani had been passing. I caught a glimpse of a man's back entering the duka next to the chai house. I could see he was wearing a suit coat. I walked toward the duka.

"Hey, Dean, are you okay?" called Dave from inside the chai house.

"Yes," I answered absently. "I just needed to get something out here."

I walked into the duka and slid along the dirty glass counter to the corner. I eyed the man who'd walked in before me. It was the same Reverend Kimani! He was buying several loaves of bread, as well as jam, sugar, flour, and some biscuits (cookies).

"You've come a long way to buy from my store," the shopkeeper said to Reverend Kimani. "There are many stores closer to your home than mine. And you're buying Mzungu (white people) food today. Are you expecting some guests?"

"Yes, yes, I know there are shops closer to my house," Reverend Kimani said. He seemed irritated. "I just came to visit my cousin who is the pastor here in Rugendo. So I decided to buy some things here since we are expecting some missionaries to visit."

I tried to slink deeper into the corner. I knew Mr. Kimani had just told a lie. Pastor Kariuki was away for a one-week evangelistic campaign at the coast. I didn't know of any missionaries who were going to visit him, but I had a pretty good idea who he might be buying the bread and jam for.

Just then the shopkeeper's son came over to where I stood. I didn't want Mr. Kimani to notice me. "Some Black Cat," I said as quietly as I could, pointing at the licorice gum.

"How many?" the young man asked. By now, I was sure Reverend Kimani would see me and recognize me. But he was fumbling with his pocket and counting out change. I pulled out two ten-cent pieces and croaked, "Two please," then snatched the gum, slipped out the door, and ran to the chai house.

"Hey, Dean, we were just getting ready to drink your chai when we noticed a horrible piece of mandazi floating in it," said Jon jokingly. Then he saw my face. "What is it, Dean? You look like you've seen a ghost."

"No time to explain," I said sitting down and gulping my chai, floating mandazi and all. Leaning forward, I whispered, "But when I give the signal, we have to leave here quietly and follow someone on our bikes."

"Is this a game?" Dave asked, not sure of the way I was acting.

"No, I'm serious," I said. "Now, act normally and do what I say. I'll explain later."

Dave and Jon just shrugged, but they did what I said.

I knew Reverend Kimani had ridden a bicycle to Rugendo because when I'd watched him in the duka I'd noticed his pants leg was tucked into his sock. All we'd have to do was watch until he got on his big black bicycle, the kind that all Kenyan men ride, and then check out which direction he took. Then we could follow at a distance. I thanked the Lord for the rain. It would be easier to follow the tracks his bike tires would make in the soft red Rugendo mud.

My mind was still trying to work out exactly why Reverend Kimani would have kidnapped Matt. He may have thought Matt could identify him as a Christian who had bowed to pressure and taken the secret oath. Perhaps he thought Matt would tell his dad and Reverend Kimani feared he would be kicked out of his pastorate. Somehow I knew Matt's kidnapping tied in with the secret oath we'd seen.

Just then I saw Reverend Kimani pass by the chai house carrying his purchases in a woven sisal basket called a kiondo. I let a few seconds pass before I leaned forward and hissed, "Outside, now! And be as inconspicuous as possible."

Both Jon and Dave raised their eyebrows at what they thought was my outrageous behavior. But we all went out. I saw Reverend Kimani just getting onto his bicycle, and then he rode off down the dirt road that eventually led to Nairobi. But there were a lot of places to turn off before Nairobi so I knew we'd have to watch closely.

"We can't lose that man," I said to Jon and Dave. "But we can't let him know we're following him, either."

"Okay," Jon said looking dubious. "But would you mind telling us what this is all about? Why are we following that man?"

"Because," I said, pausing for emphasis, "I'm convinced he's the man we saw at the oathing ceremony, and I'm sure he's the one who kidnapped Matt. But we have to follow him to prove anything. I saw him buy food and I'm positive it's for Matt to eat. We have to find out where he's hiding Matt."

CHAPTER ELEVEN

Repairing a Flat Tire

We waited until Reverend Kimani rounded the corner where the lone yellow fever tree stood before we rode off after him. Dave had thought to buy some mandazi from the chai house. We strapped the mandazi, wrapped in newspaper, to my handlebars.

We rode up to the yellow fever tree and watched Reverend Kimani's back vanishing slowly around the next bend. There was a long mud puddle in the road and we noticed where Reverend Kimani's bicycle had made tracks in the soft mud around the edges of the puddle.

On an impulse, Jon jumped down and squatted by the tire track. "It's really interesting," he said after a few seconds. "Reverend Kimani's tire must have had a bad puncture once. There's a regular square mark here that doesn't match the tire pattern. That happens sometimes when a piece of rubber is patched on the outside of the tire itself to repair a ragged tear caused by sharp rocks in the road. Anyway, with a mark like that it will be easy to identify his tracks."

Dave and I nodded wisely. I was glad Jon had the ability to notice things. I sure wouldn't have thought to look closely at the tire tracks. Nor would I have picked out what Jon had. But now that we knew, we hoped the information would be useful.

We kept following Reverend Kimani, catching glimpses of him as we came to corners. We kept well back and were quite sure he hadn't seen us yet. I knew we were getting near the village of Mkutano, where several roads crossed. In fact the name of the village, Mkutano, meant "meeting place." At first a few dukas had sprung up at Mkutano and then more houses. Now it had become a sizable village with a weekly market. I decided we needed to have a plan before we got to Mkutano, so I signaled to the other two to stop.

"We're coming up to Mkutano village," I said to Dave and Jon. "We need to decide what to do before we get there. Since we know about the square patch on Reverend Kimani's tire, it will make it a bit easier for us. When we can see the village from that hill over there, we'll wait and watch. If Reverend Kimani goes through the village and keeps going, we'll see which road he goes on. Then we can follow. But if he stops in the village, we'll lose sight of him. Then we'll have to go down and try to follow his tracks in town. We can thank the Lord for last night's rain."

We set off again, stopping when we reached a hill that overlooked Mkutano. Looking down, we saw Reverend Kimani getting close to the village. Once in the village, we lost sight of him. We waited, watching in case he would reappear on one of the other roads leading from the village. But we saw nothing. He must have entered a building. We'd have to track him.

Just then a heard a hissing sound. I reached back and pinched my rear tire. It was soft and getting softer. "Oh, no," I said. "I have a puncture. Did either of you guys bring a repair kit?"

Both Dave and Jon shook their heads. "We weren't expecting a long bike ride this morning when we went to the chai house," Dave said.

Suddenly I remembered the Black Cat gum I'd bought earlier. Pulling the gum out of my pocket I said, "I can repair my tire with this gum, at least for a while. But it will take a bit of time without tools. You guys had better go into Mkutano and trace Reverend Kimani. I'll catch up either by following his tracks or else one of you can wait for me at the crossroads in town."

Jon and Dave agreed and rode down the hill into the village. I popped the gum into my mouth and started chewing so it would be ready to seal the puncture. I started to take off my rear tire. It was almost eleven, and the burning sun had made sweat drip off my face like rain off a mabati (corrugated iron) roof. So I pulled my bike off the road and pushed it under the shade of a large cabbage tree.

Then I struggled to get my wheel off without tools. I had to bang the nuts with a rock until they were loose enough for me to undo by hand. In doing this, I scraped the skin off my knuckles, but at least I had the wheel off.

Then I tried to use a stick to stretch the tire off the rim, but the stick kept breaking. I hunted around until I found a sharp piece of obsidian rock, or volcanic glass, the debris from a volcanic eruption some centuries before. The rock was sharp on one side but thick on the other. The thick end fit nicely in my hand and I managed to force the sharp edge between the tire and the rim and soon I had the tire free and the tube out.

In the tube I found the problem. A small thorn had made a hole. I removed the thorn and then applied the licorice chewing gum to the hole. I really plastered the gum on to make sure it would hold till I got home. Then I ran my finger around the inside of the tire to be sure there were no more thorns or small rocks to cause another puncture.

I put the tube in, tucking the valve into the hole in the rim, and finally put the tire back on. Then I took out the hand pump I always carried on the frame of my bike and was just starting to pump when I heard voices on the road.

"Wi mwega, are you well, Bwana Kimani?" I heard a voice say.

Kimani? I wondered if it was our Reverend Kimani. I looked carefully. It was! What had happened to Dave and Jon? I didn't know, but I dropped to my stomach and crawled behind a bush to listen.

After sitting through so many Kikuyu church services, I understood a bit of the language. Not to speak it so much, but I could usually understand what people were saying. I heard Reverend Kimani explaining to his friend how he had just returned a bike to his brother in Mkutano. "Bike" is an easy word to pick out. It had been adapted from the English and was known as baisikeli.

"I used the baisikeli to go to Rugendo on business," Reverend Kimani was saying, "and now that I've returned it, I'm going to my shamba to check on how the maize is doing."

The two men shook hands and parted. I watched Reverend Kimani walk about twenty-five yards before turning down a narrow path. It was up to me, now, to follow him. Dave and Jon would be looking for non-existent tracks leading out of Mkutano while the bike was parked in Reverend Kimani's brother's house.

I pumped my tire as fast as I could. But I was in too much of a hurry trying to get the wheel back on and I pinched my index finger between the chain and the sprockets. I sucked my finger for a minute until it felt better. I took my finger out and looked at it. It had two nasty blood blisters.

But I had to follow Reverend Kimani. Ignoring the ache in my finger, I went back to work and finally got the wheel back on. It wobbled when I rode it because I could only hand tighten the nuts. But wobbly or not, riding my bike was faster than walking. I came to the path where Reverend Kimani had turned. Suddenly I realized I had to leave some sort of message for Dave and Jon or they wouldn't know where I'd gone.

I got off my bike and gathered stones and piled them together in what I hoped looked like an arrow pointing toward the path. Even if it wasn't the greatest arrow, I hoped it would catch Jon and Dave's attention. Then I took a stick and scratched out a message in the mud. It read, "Matt's this way. Please get help. Dean."

Satisfied with the message, I jumped onto my bike and rode down the path.

CHAPTER TWELVE

The Bike Wreck

The path narrowed and my shoulders brushed branches that clutched at me from both sides. The path led through thick forest down into one of the many ravines that scarred the hills in that area. As the path grew steeper, I began to go faster and faster. I gripped my brakes, but nothing happened. Because of my fear of hills, I had worn the brakes so thin they couldn't stop me now.

I careened down the path and the only thing I could think of to stop myself would be to crash into the bushes that choked the path. I didn't know which bushes might be filled with wickedly curved wait-a-bit thorns. Nor could I guess where the stinging nettles that infested these forests might grow. So I gripped my brakes harder and tried not to close my eyes as I belted down the path.

Suddenly I came around a corner and found myself approaching a bridge over a small river at the bottom of the ravine. On the other side of the river, the path went up. I'd made it. Except the bridge was just six narrow poles stretched over the river. The poles weren't straight and there were nasty cracks between them. And I was going too fast to stop.

Without even time to think or pray, I decided to try to cross the bridge. The other choice would have been to head my bike off a four-foot bank into the river.

My front wheel hit the bridge and I started across. But then my wheels slipped off the round pole and plunged into a crack. My bike stopped. Very quickly. But I didn't stop. I flew over the handlebars and hit the edge of the bridge. Then I found myself sitting in the foot-deep water of the river.

I looked up and saw my bike wedged between two of the bridge poles. My handle bars were bent sideways. I guess I'd been reluctant to let go when my bike stopped. I found myself panting for breath. Slowly, I stood up. My hip hurt. I seemed to remember hitting my hip on the side of the bridge. My wrist ached as well, and it had a red mark on it. Otherwise, I seemed to be okay. "Boy," I thought to myself, "I hope Jon and Dave have better brakes than I do."

After climbing up the bank of the river, I reached for a handful of leaves, checking carefully to see that they weren't stinging nettles. I used the leaves to wipe the mud off and to dry myself as best I could. Then I walked onto the bridge which was much easier to negotiate on foot. After tugging hard, I freed my bike and wheeled it onto the far side of the river. I stood in front of it and gripped the front wheel between my knees. Then I held onto the handlebars and straightened them. They felt pretty loose. I knew I'd have to get out a wrench and tighten the bolt when I got home. But now, I had to find out where Reverend Kimani had taken Matt. *If* he had taken Matt. I didn't even have any proof about that. Really, I was just guessing. *Maybe I should just go back and find Jon and Dave at Mkutano,* I thought.

I decided I'd better ask God to help me to find Matt, and to help me to not give up. I knew that even if I might be wrong, I had to keep trying. Taking my bike, I started pushing it up the path that angled steeply up the hill. Just then I heard a blue monkey give its shrill nasal alarm cry farther up the hill.

Reverend Kimani was still ahead of me. He must have startled a troop of monkeys. They traveled in groups of ten to fifteen in these hills. I knew I had to keep following. But where were Dave and Jon? If they'd only catch up soon I wouldn't feel so alone.

Alone? I'd just prayed to the Lord. I knew he was with me. He always was. But I still wished Dave and Jon would catch up. And soon! I gritted my teeth and pushed my bike up the path that was now blocked in places by big rocks that had slid down the steep hillside along with mud caused by the recent rains.

It was hot. The hill on this side of the ravine didn't have as many trees. I looked at the shadows left by the sun and judged it must be a little after noon. The sun felt like a hot hammer pounding down. The rocks radiated with the heat. But I kept pushing my bike up. Finally I arrived at the top of the hill. Ahead of me, I could see a plateau with fields of maize plants growing, young and green. Other fields had been planted in potatoes, and the plants were tall with lovely white flowers, evidence of the good rains.

I leaned my bike against a tree and scanned the horizon to find Reverend Kimani. This must have been an area recently opened up for farming because I could see only one or two small huts. They were shelters, built to shield against the midday sun when the farmers came to dig on their land. But the people lived in villages like Mkutano on the other side of the ridge.

As I looked down, I saw a man moving toward one of the small huts. I marked it in my mind as about halfway between a wild olive tree and a large boulder. I could see the path tracing down to the plateau. At this distance I couldn't tell for sure if it was Reverend Kimani, but since I could see no other sign of life, I assumed it must be him. And what better place to hide Matt? I began to get nervous. My stomach felt all wiggly, as if flying ants were tickling my insides with their long, feathery wings.

I decided I should wait for a while, hoping Dave and Jon would catch up. If they didn't, it would be easier to sneak down to the hut later in the afternoon as it got dark.

Suddenly I felt hungry. I remembered the mandazis tied to my handle bars. I unstrapped them and started to eat. Cold grease oozed out as I bit into them. But when you're hungry, even a cold mandazi tastes good.

As I sat in the shade by my bike, eating, I suddenly heard a crashing sound in the trees behind me.

CHAPTER THIRTEEN

Blue Monkeys

The crashing noise startled me. Was Reverend Kimani rushing at me? Or was a Cape buffalo charging at me through the brush? I had shinnied halfway up the nearest tree before I realized where the noise came from.

As I reached for a branch, I looked up and saw the trees were swaying with the weight of a troop of blue monkeys. A few of them jumped from tree to tree, clutching the ends of branches, hanging and kicking as they scrabbled for a better grip. Then, regaining their balance, they would leap again. Others leaned with their backs against the trunks of trees and stared at me.

I felt foolish. *My imagination is running wild,* I thought. I realized these must be the monkeys I had heard earlier, screeching at

Reverend Kimani. Reverend Kimani had probably thrown a rock or something at them to keep them from coming too close to the shambas, or small farms on the plateau.

The monkeys settled down and looked at me. I began to lose my grip on the tree. My arm muscles were tired and I found I had scraped my knees. I slowly slid down the tree.

Now that I was on the ground, the monkeys became uneasy again and began chattering. They sounded rather like birds chirping. But I didn't want to scare them. If I did, they might scream with their loud EEE-yonk cry. That sound carried for miles, and Reverend Kimani would know someone else was nearby. If he did have Matt in the hut, he would be alert. He might even take Matt somewhere else.

As I thought about what to do, I remembered my half-eaten mandazi. Moving slowly so I wouldn't frighten the monkeys, I edged over to where I had dropped the mandazi in my frantic scramble up the tree. Then I broke it into several small pieces. I didn't dare throw the pieces to the monkeys. They'd think I was throwing rocks, and they'd make noise for sure. I slowly walked along, placing pieces of mandazi below the trees where the monkeys sat. My unhurried motions must have calmed them, because the chatter died down.

After laying out the pieces of mandazi, I returned to my bike and sat down. I looked down onto the plateau. But without turning my head too far, I could still see the monkeys out of the corner of my eye.

For about ten minutes nothing happened. Then curiosity took over. A big monkey began to clamber slowly down from his perch.

The big monkey hopped to the ground and cautiously crept up to the closest piece of mandazi. Sitting down beside it, the monkey gingerly picked it up and examined it. Then he sniffed at it. Apparently he didn't like the smell of the oil it had been fried in because he wrinkled up his nose and dropped the mandazi. But after a few minutes he reached for it again. This time he nibbled at it. The taste must have been better than the smell because after the first nibble, he stuffed the rest of the piece into his mouth. This signaled the rest of the monkeys. Within seconds they had swooped down to the ground and eaten up all the pieces of mandazi. Then they all looked at me and began coming closer to me. I guess they wanted more.

I showed them my empty hands in a gesture I hoped showed them I didn't have anything else. They didn't understand and kept edging closer. Now what could I do? Climbing a tree wouldn't help. I knew monkeys didn't normally attack people, but I was alone and their teeth looked sharp.

I began to pray. It seemed I always turned to the Lord as a last resort. Maybe that's the way most people are.

As the big male came within three feet, my heartbeat must have tripled. Then I saw the newspaper that the mandazi had been wrapped in. I took it and tossed it as far as I could. The monkeys all scrambled after it, drawn by its shape and the oil that soaked it.

While the monkeys were occupied, I jumped onto my bike and pedaled a safe distance away from the trees. About one hundred yards away I came to a big boulder. I turned my bike into the shade and got off and looked back. The monkeys were still tearing up the newspaper. I knew these monkeys didn't like to go too far from trees so I hoped I would be safe. After a few minutes they tired of the newspaper. They looked briefly in my direction, but then the big male climbed a tree and I could see and hear branches crashing as the troop retreated back into the forest.

I took a big breath in relief and thanked God for helping me to think of the newspaper. Then I prayed that God would bring Dave and Jon to find me and that He would help us to find Matt. Feeling better, I sat down in the shade of the boulder.

I had a good view of the plateau. I could see wisps of smoke rising from the hut where Reverend Kimani had entered. It meant he had started a cook fire. If Matt was there, he wouldn't be starving to death.

I sat for a long time. Now it was getting late and the sun began to dip behind the volcanic mountains to the west. I started to devise a plan to rescue Matt. I would wait about another half-hour. Then I would sneak down to the hut on foot. If Matt was there I would rescue him and we'd run to my bike and ride double back to the road—if my chewing gum-patched tire could handle the load. And what about Reverend Kimani? I couldn't overpower him. I thought and thought but could find no answer to that problem. *Well,* I thought, *I'll solve that problem later. Somehow.*

Just then I heard a rattling sound from behind me. Instinctively, I ducked down and hid myself from view. Within seconds a bike whizzed by. It was Jon. I jumped up. "Jon,

Jon!" I called.

Jon whirled his head around and on seeing me his face broke into a grin. Braking to a stop he came back to me. "Dean, am I ever glad to see you," he began.

I motioned to him to talk quietly and then we sat down together behind the boulder. I told him how I'd followed Reverend Kimani and how I felt sure he had Matt held in a hut below us.

Jon told me how he and Dave had followed Reverend Kimani's bike tracks into Mkutano. "But we lost the tracks in town. We waited for a while in case Reverend Kimani was drinking tea and might see us and be suspicious. We bought some sodas at a kiosk while we waited. Then we searched every road leading out of Mkutano and couldn't find the tire tracks anywhere.

"We were just about to give up and go back and pick you up to go home when Dave noticed a big, black bike leaning against a house. We decided to have a closer look. Sure enough, it turned out to be the bike with a tire that had a big, oblong patch on the outside. After asking a few questions we learned that the bike had recently been returned, and Reverend Kimani had gone to check on his maize field. The man who told us had pointed with his chin in this direction and said the fields were on the other side of the ridge. So we rode back up the road to find you."

"Did you find my sign?" I asked.

Jon laughed. "It wasn't too hard. It looked like a roadblock, there were so many stones!"

"Sorry," I said. "I just didn't want you to miss it. But where's Dave?"

"Well, your message said to get help, so Dave rode home to get some of the men from Rugendo. And I came to see if I could catch up with you."

"How'd you do on the bridge at the bottom of the ravine?" I asked.

"I stopped and walked my bike over," Jon answered. "It wasn't too tough. Why?"

I told him about my crash and then showed him the purple bruise on my hip. We Rhinos always compared bruises, cuts, and scars.

"That's a great bruise," Jon said whistling softly. "I'd rate it a 9.8, even better than Matt's when he fell off the rope swing."

Mentioning Matt brought my mind back to the present. "When do you think our dads will get here?" I asked Jon.

"Soon, I hope," he answered. And we

both decided to wait until they came.

But then I saw movement near the hut. "It looks like Reverend Kimani," I whispered. We watched as the figure moved away from the hut.

"I wonder where he's going?" Jon asked.

"I don't know," I answered. "But if he's not in the hut, I think maybe we should go down now and get Matt. Otherwise, even with our dads, someone might get hurt if we have to force our way in."

Jon agreed. We prayed quietly for God to be with us. Then we ran down the path toward the hut, crouched over so Reverend Kimani would have a hard time seeing us even if he looked up.

CHAPTER FOURTEEN

Rev. Kumani's Story

Jon and I raced down the path toward the hut. We had to hurry. The sun touched the peaks and we knew we barely had half an hour of daylight left.

When we reached the hut, we hid behind a bush to catch our breath and listen. We could hear no sound from inside. Hoping it was safe, we crept to the low door and peered in. We saw Matt! He wasn't tied at all, though a sisal rope lay coiled nearby. He sat on a three-legged stool in the corner. This would be an easy rescue.

On seeing us, his mouth opened wide. "Dean! Jon! Boy, am I ever glad to see you guys!"

We hurried in. I was dying to ask questions but I knew we had to get out quickly.

"Where did Reverend Kimani go?" I asked. "When will he get back?"

"He want to fetch water. But how'd you find out his name was Reverend Kimani? And how did you trace me here?"

"I'll tell you later," I said. "Right now we have to get you out of here and back home safely."

"But I can't leave without saying goodbye to Reverend Kimani," Matt said. "He'd be worried and wonder what had happened."

"What's wrong with your head?" Jon burst out. "The man kidnapped you and has held you hostage for three days. Now we have a chance to make a break for it and you want to wait and tell him goodbye? Come on, let's go!"

"I tell you, I can't," Matt said, pleadingly. "You see, Reverend Kimani is no criminal. Yes, he kidnapped me. But now I understand he did it out of fear. I can't just leave. I need to talk with him before we go."

"We have to get you out of here now," I argued. "It's almost dark, which is probably why he left you untied. He thought you wouldn't risk going through the forest by yourself at night. But now there's three of us. Come on." I grabbed Matt's hand and, being bigger than he was, I pulled him up and dragged him toward the door.

Just then the door filled up with Reverend Kimani. He held a plastic container full of water. On seeing us he dropped the water container and stepped forward. "What's going on here?" he asked.

I wanted to push past him and run but the doorway was small and I wasn't sure what would happen if Reverend Kimani stopped me. Besides, I couldn't leave Matt. I stepped back and put an arm protectively around Matt.

Matt spoke up. "These are two of my friends, Reverend Kimani. They came to rescue me and take me home. But I refused to leave without talking to you first." Matt motioned to us to sit down, which we did.

Reverend Kimani said slowly, "I will boil some tea and we will talk." He poured some water in a black-bottomed cooking pot and placed it over the cooking fire, which had a few red coals left. Then he blew on the fire and added a few pieces of firewood. Once, as he bent over the fire, I was tempted to leap on him and try to hold him down. But Matt saw my look and he shook his head. I didn't understand why Matt didn't want us to rescue him, but I decided to play along with him. After all, he was our leader.

Reverend Kimani sat back. "Well, boys," he said, "did Matt explain to you why I brought him here?"

"No," I said. "We only got here a little before you did. We wanted to get out of here before you got back. But Matt insisted..."

"Ah, yes," said Reverend Kimani. "Matt would insist. God has really used this young boy to change my heart. Let me tell you my story. I am a pastor to about five churches in this area. My home is just on the other side of Mkutano. God gave me the ability to preach well. As a result, my name became well known in this area and around the country. Many people talked about the beautiful sermons I preached. I am often invited to speak at seminars and youth camps. In fact, it was at one of those seminars that I first met Matt and his father."

I listened closely. This didn't sound like the voice of a kidnapper. A glance out the door showed me the sun had gone completely. I settled back. We might be here all night.

Mr. Kimani continued. "Satan used my speaking ability to trap me. He whispered in my ear that I was a great preacher. I believed him. I became proud. No one could teach me anything. I began to look down on the other pastors in the area and be critical of them. Yes, Satan trapped me with my own pride."

Mr. Kimani leaned forward and poured some milk from a bottle into the boiling water. Then he sprinkled in some tea leaves and the mixture turned a golden brown. He signaled to Matt who gave him a brown paper bag. Reverend Kimani shook sugar from this bag into the tea. Then with a big wooden spoon, he gently stirred the Kenyan chai.

Sitting back, he went on. "A few months ago, with the announcement of countrywide elections for our members of parliament, the Kikuyu elders began enforcing oathing. This is when people in my tribe are forced to join with others in sacrificing a goat. They then take an oath of loyalty to the tribe. The purpose is political, which isn't so bad, but in the oath we have to swear by the spirits and gods of our past tribal religion. As Christians, we had to oppose this. A Christian taking the oath is seen as denying Christ. I was the loudest in the fight. But you see, I fought the battle in my own strength alone. I had forgotten to turn to the Lord for help.

"Then one night I had a visit from the Kikuyu elders and our local mundu mugo. They told me I had to take the oath the next day. I wanted to say no, but suddenly I was very afraid. The witch doctor threatened curses on my wife and on my children. If I had been walking closely to the Lord, I would have turned to Him and resisted, knowing that Jesus is more powerful than Satan and any of his evil spirits. But because of my pride, I had stopped turning to the Lord for anything. I tried to do everything by my own power. But my strength failed me, and I agreed to go."

"Then it *was* you we saw that day near Rugendo," I said.

"Yes," he answered sadly. "And when I saw Matt, I was sure he'd recognized me. I thought he would tell his father and I would be thrown out of the church. I was so afraid I just wanted to make sure no one found out how I had failed the Lord.

"Then I visited my cousin, the pastor at Rugendo, to make arrangements for when I was scheduled to preach there the next Sunday. As I left Rugendo, I saw you boys on your bicycles and, on an impulse, I decided to follow you. I went into the forest. When I saw you returning, I hid."

"I was right, then," I interrupted. Turning to Matt I said, "I told you I saw someone that day when we first rode up the old slave trail." Matt nodded. Then we both looked at Reverend Kimani.

Reverend Kimani continued, "I didn't think any of you had seen me. But when I preached the next Sunday, I was so afraid. I saw Matt sitting there and I felt certain he would tell his dad he'd seen me at the oathing ceremony."

Matt shook his head. "I had to confess to Reverend Kimani this afternoon that I wasn't paying much attention to the sermon that day. I was busy counting holes in the church rafters made by wood-boring beetles. To tell the truth, I'd almost forgotten about the oathing ceremony."

Reverend Kimani went on. "That afternoon, I heard my cousin's son, Ben, talking about a bike race. I knew you boys were involved. I looked at the map of the race. I remembered a place I'd seen in the woods the day I'd followed you and I thought it would be the perfect chance to kidnap Matt. I wasn't sure what I'd do after I had him. I didn't want to hurt him, but I had to make sure he didn't speak. You can see I was desperate.

"I hid Matt here. But I had no idea what to do next. I ran out of food so I left Matt tied up this morning and borrowed a bike to go buy some food for him at the Rugendo duka. I didn't dare buy things in Mkutano. People might have been suspicious. But today has been so hard. I have felt so guilty and I didn't know what to do. So when I got back and gave Matt some food, I told him the whole story. I was amazed when he forgave me completely."

I looked at Matt, his eyes staring at the floor. I guessed he was embarrassed. Matt looked up. "I told Reverend Kimani we all make mistakes, but God forgives us if we admit we've sinned and pray for forgiveness. I quoted 1 John 1:9, which we learned a few weeks ago in Sunday school. I also reminded him about how Peter denied Jesus, too. Not once, but three times. But Jesus forgave him and used him.

"Just this afternoon Reverend Kimani prayed and confessed his sin, first for taking the oath and then for kidnapping me to cover up his sin. But as he prayed, he became convicted of his pride and lack of trust in the Lord. And when he had confessed that and stood up, I knew he was a changed man. Then he went to get some water for our tea and you guys showed up to rescue me. Now you know why I couldn't leave."

Jon and I nodded. It was quite a story. Reverend Kimani began passing out enamel mugs of tea. It was sweet and good.

"So how did you guys find me?" Matt asked. We told him our story. Reverend Kimani laughed quietly when we told about following the unique track made by the bicycle he had borrowed.

Just then we heard barking and voices outside. Looking out we saw an army of lights coming down the hill. "Dave must have brought everyone from Rugendo," Jon said.

Reverend Kimani's eyes opened wide with fear. "I don't like dogs," he said.

Matt held his arm gently. "Don't worry, Reverend Kimani. We'll make sure nothing happens to you."

Then we stepped out and called, "We're over here."

CHAPTER FIFTEEN

Reunion

Within minutes the missionaries and Kenyans from Rugendo reached the hut. Matt's mom and dad led the way. Seeing Matt, they rushed in and hugged him. Usually we Rhinos aren't much for tears or hugs, but this night they seemed to come naturally. When I saw Matt's mom hugging him, I started to cry with happiness. She kept repeating, "Matt! You're safe! You're safe!"

Then I was enveloped in my father's strong arms. I hugged him back. "I see you found your friend," he said. I nodded through my tears. My mom joined in as well and the three of us stood hugging each other.

I noticed that Reverend Kimani stood away from the crowd. It seemed like he wanted to disappear in the shadows. But he didn't try to run away. I knew his repentance was true. No matter what happened, he would accept it.

After several minutes, Matt's dad stood back and looked around. Seeing Reverend Kimani, he asked, "Did you help rescue Matt? Where's the man who kidnapped my son? Did he escape or do you have him tied up in the hut?"

Reverend Kimani could only look at the ground. I could tell his heart was heavy. Then taking a deep breath, he looked up and began, "I have something to confess to all of you. I am the one who kidnapped Matt."

Shocked silence followed Reverend Kimani's confession. My dad responded first. "You? What do you mean? Surely you didn't..." His voice trailed off.

With tears in his eyes, Reverend Kimani repeated his story. At the end of it, Matt's dad stepped forward and embraced Reverend Kimani. "What you did has hurt us very much. You don't know how worried we've been about our son. But we can learn from our children. If Matt has forgiven you, we forgive you, too. I am sure God will use this to bring about good in our lives and in your life as well. Come on, let's get back to Rugendo."

And with that, we began the hike back to the road where the cars had been left. All the way home, I kept thinking, *Matt is safe. God really did answer our prayers.*

• • •

About a month later, we had a club meeting in our tree house. Matt opened in prayer and then told us about his visit to Reverend Kimani in prison. Matt's parents hadn't pressed any charges. But the Kenyan police had been appalled by the kidnapping. Such a thing had never happened in the country before and they felt if there was no punishment it might lead to further kidnappings. So they had insisted Reverend Kimani be charged.

After the trial, Reverend Kimani received his sentence of five years in prison and ten strokes with the kiboko, a hippo-hide whip. Matt had even gotten to testify and he had asked the judge not to be too harsh, as Reverend Kimani had treated him well.

Reverend Kimani accepted his sentence. He had said to Matt and his parents, "When we sin, we must pay the penalty. God has forgiven me. But there are still consequences I must endure because of my sin. I am ready to accept them. I know God will use this prison sentence to glorify him and to help me overcome my pride."

My dad had written an article about the kidnapping and trial and Reverend Kimani's comments for the magazine. Already that article had brought in a lot of letters. People who had read it were impressed by Reverend Kimani's attitude, and many had written to say they were turning to the Lord as a result of Reverend Kimani's testimony.

Now Matt had gone to visit Reverend Kimani in prison. "It's amazing how the Lord is using that man," he said. "In prison he has started four Bible studies and already thirty men have prayed to receive Jesus as their Savior. And he says he is determined to serve the Lord as long as he's in prison and when he's released. But he doesn't speak with pride. Instead he says he is amazed how God can still use him after the way he acted."

"I guess your kidnapping did work out for the best after all," I said. "But we sure didn't feel that way when we were still searching for you. It's really amazing how God keeps his promise in Romans 8:28 that all things work together for good for people who love God."

Then we bowed our heads and thanked

God for Matt's safety and for working in Reverend Kimani's heart.

After praying, we sat quietly for a while. Then Matt spoke up. "You know, Dean, I don't think your victory in our bike safari was really fair. After all, I never got a chance to ride further than the first bend. I suggest we stage another race."

"Another race!" Jon said standing up.

"Yeah, that would be great!" Dave agreed.

"You're right, Matt," I said. "I never felt right about winning that race anyway." And we began making preparations for our second bicycle safari.

THE RUGENDO RHINOS
AND

CHAPTER ONE

Mzima Springs

"Over there! I see them. Five elephants and they're on my side," I said, looking over at my little brother, Craig. "That puts me ahead, ten to four."

"But it's not fair, Mom," Craig pleaded. "Dean always wins these contests because he's better at spotting elephants than I am. And anyway, it's not fair because they're all on your side, Dean. Trade you sides, no trade backs."

Looking ahead, I could see a few red shapes among the baobab trees. "Sure I'll trade," I said, and we swapped seats. As soon as I'd sat down, I said, "Four more elephants for me."

"You cheated, Dean! You cheated!" Craig said loudly, starting to pound on my shoulder. "Those are really on *my* side. I didn't mean to trade sides. I still get to count those."

"You said no trade backs," I reminded him. "Remember?"

"Stop fighting, you two," Dad said, braking our car to a stop right by the elephants and taking out his camera. "What amazes me," he went on, "is how red the elephants get here in Tsavo Game Park. Elephants are normally gray, but here they're always a bright orange-red. It comes from the red dirt in the area. Oh, look!"

One of the elephants had just sucked some of the red dust into his trunk and began taking a dust shower. Dad turned the car off so the engine vibrations wouldn't jiggle his camera. He was so busy clicking off pictures he didn't notice one of the elephants edging toward us. But Mom noticed.

"That elephant is coming closer, dear. Please start the car and let's get going. You know it bothers me when you turn the engine off next to dangerous animals."

Dad smiled. "Don't worry, he's not mad, just curious." But the elephant looked very big and I was pleased when Dad started the car and we drove away.

We were on our way to have a two-week vacation at Mombasa on the Indian Ocean.

My parents worked as missionaries at Rugendo mission station in Kenya. Once a year we'd travel the three hundred hot miles to spend some time at the coast. I was really excited, because this year all the Rhinos would be there at the same time.

I don't mean real rhinos with horns. I mean my best friends from Rugendo. Matt Chadwick, Dave Krenden, and Jon Freedman. The four of us had formed a club and we always did everything together. Matt was our leader and he had named us the Rhinos because it sounded good with Rugendo. My name is Dean Sandler and I'd been elected secretary of the club, even though my handwriting looked more like the crab scratchings that etched the white sands of Diani Beach, where we'd be spending our vacation. Since my dad was a magazine editor, the others figured I'd know something about writing. We Rhinos had built a tree house where we held our club meetings. We went bird hunting together, played soccer, and rode our bikes. We even organized a bicycle race which we called a bike safari. But that was another adventure.

Anyway, there was a place near Mombasa where missionaries could rent cottages cheaply. Of course the cottages were a little run down. They had grass-thatched roofs that leaked, rusty plumbing, and lots of bats. But we didn't mind, because we spent most of our time in the warm ocean water or on the beach.

Matt, Dave, and Jon had gone down with their parents a few days before. We'd had to wait because my dad wanted to make sure the press finished printing the Christian magazine he edits. To make up for leaving later, my parents had decided to spend a night on the way in Tsavo Game Park. That's where we were now, driving toward the banda, or self-service cottage, we had booked at Kitani Lodge.

"How many elephants have you counted?" my dad asked, breaking into my thoughts.

"Fourteen all together," I answered.

"Yeah," said Craig, "but he cheated and four of those elephants are really mine."

"Actually," my dad said, "I'm sad we've only seen fourteen. This park used to be crowded with elephants. Just a few years ago, both of you would be in the hundreds by now and have lost track no matter which side of the car you sat on. But a few dry years left too many elephants trying to eat too little food and a lot of them starved. And now the few that remain are being hunted by poachers."

"Poachers? What are they?" asked Craig. "A kind of animal?"

Dad laughed. "They're people who shoot elephants just so they can sell the tusks to be carved into ivory jewelry and things."

The dirt road turned suddenly into bumpy washboard, and my dad had to hold tightly to the steering wheel. In the back seat, I felt as if my teeth were being rattled loose.

I saw a wooden sign that read: MZIMA SPRINGS—5 miles.

"Dad, can we go there and see the hippos?" I asked.

He looked at his watch. "It's about three," he said. "Tell you what. The hippos will still be sleeping now. Let's go to our banda first. It's only about four more miles down this road. We can unpack, sit in the shade for a while, and have a cold drink. Then at about 5:30 we can drive to Mzima Springs. Animals will be out then and maybe we'll see the hippos coming up out of the water."

We bounced the final few miles to Kitani Lodge, a collection of eight or so wooden bandas with iron roofs tucked away under some giant yellow fever trees. After checking in, we parked next to our banda and unloaded the car. Some baboons lazed under the trees in front of the house and eyed our food boxes greedily.

After unloading, my dad opened the ice chest he'd packed early that morning and pulled out cold bottles of soda pop. But he'd forgotten a bottle opener. We found one in the banda's set of utensils, but it was so rusty, it bent without opening the first bottle.

"Dean," he said, "where's your Swiss army knife with all the gadgets. I need you to open the bottles. I'm thirsty."

I had to confess I'd left my knife at home in Rugendo. It was my prize possession and I rarely left home without it. But on trips to Mombasa, I was afraid the salt water and high humidity would ruin it. "But I know how to open the bottles without an opener," I said, trying to redeem myself. Taking a bottle, I went to the door and inserted the cap in the edge of the door where the tongue held the door shut. Then I popped off the top and handed it to my dad.

"Thanks," he said. "Where'd you learn to do that?"

I just shrugged and took the other bottles and opened them. Then we sat down on the veranda to rest for a while.

It was hot and we could see the heat rising in wiggly lines above the tall yellow grass that stretched out in front of us. "Right over there," my dad said, pointing in the distance, "is Mount Kilimanjaro."

"I don't see it," said Craig, shading his eyes with his hands and staring at the mound of white clouds on the horizon.

"It's covered with clouds now. The best time to see the mountain is early in the morning. It's the highest mountain in Africa."

We played a game of Rook while we waited for the afternoon to cool down. Then, a little after five, we piled into our car and drove to Mzima Springs.

At Mzima Springs water welled up from under old black lava flows. The nearby volcanic Chyulu Hills funneled all the rain water to this one point, making it a bright green garden in the brownish plains.

I had heard there were lots of hippos at Mzima. The water was crystal clear and the game park authorities had built a glass-sided underwater tank where you could walk down and watch the hippos under the water. I'd wanted to visit the place ever since I'd first heard about it.

As we stepped out of the car, I read out loud a big warning sign: "CAUTION: You are likely to meet dangerous animals on this trail. Please proceed quietly and carefully at your own risk. The National Parks are not responsible for any eventuality."

"What does event, uh, event-whatever-you-said mean?" asked Craig.

"That means if a lion eats you it's your own fault," I said.

"Dean!" my mom spoke harshly. "What a thing to say!" Warning signs always made her nervous.

"But that's what it means, doesn't it, Dad?" I asked.

"Loosely translated, I guess you're right. But don't worry, the park always has rangers on duty here with rifles in case there's a problem."

As if on cue, two Kenyans wearing green uniforms stood up from behind a tree where they'd been chatting in the shade. Hefting rifles, they approached us.

"Jambo, jambo," they greeted.

"Hatujambo," my dad answered back, meaning we were all fine.

He talked to them in Swahili for a few minutes. I translated for Mom and Craig. "They're saying there's a lot of hippos in the pool and even a few crocodiles."

Dad turned to me. "Dean, run and get a

few magazines from the car. These men both know how to read. And their days get long." He threw me the car keys.

I got the magazines, and both men had settled down at the base of a tree and were deep in reading before we moved down the path to the hippo pool.

"It amazes me the power a magazine has over people, especially in lonely places like this," my dad said.

It made me feel good inside, too.

A five-minute walk led us to the edge of the pool. We could hear hippos blowing and grunting as we got close. Craig ran ahead and saw them first. "There they are!" he shouted.

"Quiet," I said. "Didn't you hear me read the sign to proceed quietly?"

"Sorry," he whispered. "I got excited and forgot. There, do you see them? Those flat, black shapes next to the papyrus? They look like rocks, but I saw one lift his nostrils out and breathe. And then he twitched his ears."

We saw about six hippos grouped together. When Mom and Dad caught up, we pointed them out.

"I saw them first," Craig said proudly.

"Good for you," my dad answered. "Come on up ahead here and we'll go down into the tank and watch them underwater."

A small bridge went out from the pool's edge to the tank, which was partially submerged. Craig and I scampered across the bridge and down the steps. It was like stepping into another world. Fish swam next to the glass walls. And off in the distance we could see the dim shape of a hippo moving toward the tank.

"Look at that!" I exclaimed. "Here comes a hippo and he looks like he's doing a ballet. I would have expected him to waddle. But he barely touches the bottom with his toes and then glides along."

Mom and Dad joined us in the tank and we pointed wildly at the passing hippos. They nodded. Soon other hippos joined the first one. We watched, entranced, until they had all passed by.

We wanted to see a crocodile, too, but none came. Dad said it was getting late and we'd better get back to the car. "Hippos come out of the water in the evening to feed on grass, so we'd better not stay much longer."

But Craig and I pleaded. "Please, Dad, we haven't seen a crocodile yet." Dad had pity and, against his better judgment, let us stay a bit longer. We had no luck. Finally Dad said,

"Let's go. We don't want the rangers to start worrying about us."

Reluctantly, we turned to go. Mom and Dad led the way back to the car. Craig and I kept looking back at the pool. It seemed like such a magical place.

"There!" said Craig suddenly, pointing. "I'll bet that's a crocodile." We stood and stared at the shape on the bank across the pool. It didn't move, but maybe...

Suddenly we heard a loud crashing sound from the bush between us and the car!

CHAPTER TWO

Watch for Charging Hippos!

Craig and I whirled around to see where the noise came from. Reeds, grass, and bushes waved madly. Then, not more than ten yards away from us, a hippo burst out of the bushes and charged straight at us. I started to dodge to one side, my heart beating so wildly it felt like my ears would break. But I saw Craig glued to the path. In his panic, he couldn't move!

In seconds Craig would be trampled by the hippo if he didn't move. So, without thinking, I turned back into the path of the onrushing hippo and made a diving rugby tackle on Craig. My shoulder hit him square on his ribs and we tumbled together into the grass. I felt something hit my foot. I turned to see the back side of the hippo rushing down the bank and then a big splash as he hit the water.

Craig was crying. "Mom! Dad!" I shouted. "Help! We almost got killed by a hippo!"

Dad reached us first. He knelt down and asked if we were hurt. "My ribs hurt," Craig said. But he'd stopped crying.

Dad felt the ribs tenderly. "Nothing feels broken," he reported. "Probably just bruised."

We put our arms around each other and started back to the car. I couldn't help limping. Mom noticed right away. "What's wrong with your foot?" she asked.

"It must have been bumped by the hippo after I tackled Craig," I said. "I seem to remember something hitting me."

"Probably the hippo's shoulder," Dad said. "Well, we certainly have something to pray and thank the Lord for today."

He gave both of us a squeeze.

"What I can't figure out," Mom said, "is where those two game rangers are. They're supposed to prevent this kind of thing from happening."

We came to the tree where we'd left the rangers. They were both still reading the magazines we'd given them. When Dad told them what had happened, they jumped up and apologized and asked us if we had been hurt. They said they usually went down by the pool at about this time each day to make sure no hippos came out of the water until all the visitors had left.

"But these magazines," said one. "We were just reading and we forgot about everything else. Especially this story of the man who became a Christian after being gored by a buffalo. We began to think, and in talking to each other, we decided we want to be Christians, too."

Even though Craig and I still trembled from our close call, we felt God's presence as Dad explained to the two rangers how to accept the Lord Jesus into their lives. They both prayed right there. Dad got their addresses and promised to send each of them a Bible and the name of a nearby pastor to help them.

They walked us to our car as darkness dropped like a curtain, apologizing for the hippo attack and excitedly asking questions about becoming Christians. We could hear crunching noises around us. "Hippos," the rangers explained. "They usually don't bother people. But if by mistake you get between a hippo and his water hole, he'll turn and run straight for the pool, knocking down everything in his way. He thinks you're trying to keep him away from the water where he is most comfortable."

"That's what happened to us, all right," I

said. We waved goodbye and drove back to Kitani.

As we drove through the dark, we kept seeing eyes glowing in the road as our headlights caught animals in their glare. The eyes moved crazily as the animals bounded out of our way.

A generator coughed and burped out electricity when we got back to Kitani Lodge, just enough to light one dim yellow bulb on the veranda of each banda and attract every bug in the area. Mom heated a pot of chili, so we were ready to eat in a hurry. After our day on the road and dodging hippos, it tasted extra good, as long as you didn't mind swatting away the bugs.

Mosquitoes began to swarm under the table, declaring war on all uncovered legs and ankles. After supper Mom retreated to her bed under a mosquito net to read. Craig went to bed, too. Dad motioned for me to go in and I followed him.

"Before everyone goes to sleep, I think we need to pray and thank God for safety today," he said. So, quietly and thankfully, we each prayed in turn. God does watch over us. I was convinced of that.

Dad and I went back out on the porch and, turning out the light, listened to hyenas whooping in the distance. We also heard a lion roaring. The air buzzed with the sound of insects. Listening to the sounds of an African night always relaxed me. And I liked sitting alone with my dad. We talked a little. But mostly we listened. Listened to God through his creation.

Finally we went to bed. Craig woke us up in the morning by getting out of bed and pulling the curtain back. "I see it, Dad," he said. "Just like you said. It's beautiful!"

We all stumbled sleepily out of bed to see majestic Mount Kilimanjaro, topped with snow, towering over the plains. "Wow!" was all I could say.

Dad already had his camera out and walked out the door to take some pictures. Craig went with him, asking all kinds of questions about how the camera worked and why there could be ice on the mountain when it was so hot outside.

I helped Mom get breakfast ready. After putting the cereal out on the table on the veranda, I put some bananas out and went in to get some bread. When I came out I saw a baboon hopping off the veranda with the bananas. "Hey!" I shouted and ran after the baboon. The baboon casually split open the first banana, took a bite, and then put it down on the ground and retreated.

I thought I could still get some of the

bananas back so I followed. The baboon opened another, took one bite, and put it down on the ground and ran away again. When he started opening a third banana, I knew I'd never win. Dad tried to stifle his giggling long enough to get a picture. "I guess there won't be any bananas with breakfast today," I said, walking back to the banda.

The baboon followed, picking up the bananas he'd bitten and put down.

He sat and watched us eat our breakfast. But we were careful not to leave the table unguarded.

After breakfast, we set off for the coast. We still had to drive about forty miles through the park before reaching the main road, so Craig and I began our elephant counting again.

I agreed to start at zero instead of counting the results from the previous day.

Since it was early, we saw quite a few animals. Buffaloes, giraffes, impalas, even some tiny dik-diks, a kind of antelope scarcely larger than a rabbit. But our elephant contest was tied at 0-0.

Then Dad saw some vultures circling in the sky ahead of us. "Look at that," he said. "Those vultures have spotted something dead. Maybe it's a pride of lions with a kill."

As we got closer, I commented, "Most of the birds seem to be landing. So if it's a lion kill, the lions must have moved on and left the remains for the birds and the hyenas. That's too bad. I really wanted to see some lions."

The birds were landing behind a large bush. It was a little ways off the road, so Dad had to drive the car carefully to avoid wart hog holes and low-lying thorn bushes that could easily puncture the car's tires.

Coming around the bush we found what had attracted the vultures.

CHAPTER THREE

Mombasa

At first we could only see a large, gray mound. Vultures swarmed over it, squawking and fighting, making it impossible to identify what they were picking apart. Dad stopped the car and rolled down his window.

"Phew! It stinks!" Craig said. "Let's get out of here!"

"What is it, Dad?" I asked.

"I think it's a dead elephant," he said. Then he opened his door and reached down without getting out and picked up a rock. It's against the law to get out of your car in a game park in Kenya except at designated spots, such as Mzima Springs. He threw the rock at the cluster of vultures. Startled, they flew up, revealing the sad sight.

"It's an elephant, all right," I said. "Or it

was. But what happened to it? Why doesn't it have any feet?"

"Poachers." Dad spat the word out like a curse. Then he shook his head and dug out his camera.

"You're not going to take pictures of this horrible scene, are you?" Mom asked.

"Yeah!" agreed Craig. "Let's just get out of here. It stinks so bad I'm going to throw up!"

But Dad started clicking pictures, saying, "Maybe if some of these pictures are printed in a wildlife magazine, some money can be raised to help stop this kind of thing. Ugly as this is, people have to know about it."

I watched carefully as he zoomed in on specific parts. The legs where the feet had been chopped off to make wastebaskets. The face where the ivory tusks had been chopped out. And the tail which had been cut off to make souvenir bracelets from the wire-like black hair.

The vultures began to feast again. Dad took a few more pictures and then sighed, "What a tragedy. That elephant was killed for a few cheap ornaments. Don't we humans value God's creation any more than that?"

Dad turned the car back onto the road

muttering, "Left to rot and be picked apart by vultures. Terrible."

Within minutes the rotting elephant was behind us. But the memory was branded in my mind. I knew people were sometimes desperate for money, but to kill an elephant?

"How much money would those guys get for the ivory and stuff off that elephant?" I asked.

"Not much," my dad replied. "It's worth a lot on the black market, where it's sold illegally on the coast and smuggled out of the country. But it's the black market dealers and smugglers who make all the money. The poachers get so little that they are forced to kill another elephant. Actually, if a poacher got the money the ivory was worth he could retire for life after killing just one elephant."

"Elephants on my side!" Craig burst out. "Count them, Dean. Sometimes I get mixed up when there's more than ten."

I counted twenty-two. We stopped and watched. They approached the road and marched by less than fifty yards from our car, almost gracefully in their lilting, lumbering movements.

"They're beautiful," I whispered. "And it's so much nicer to see them alive."

Dad started off again. A few flies had

flown in our open windows and they buzzed around the back seat. Craig and I declared war on them, smashing them against the windows, now closed to keep out the fine red dust.

"You'll have to clean up the windows wherever you've smashed a fly," Mom warned. That stopped us pretty quickly. We rolled down the windows and swished the flies out with our ragged, often-read comic books.

We came to the park gate. We'd seen no other elephants. I was going to lose the elephant counting contest. But then I had a thought. "Well, Craig," I announced solemnly, "it looks like we tied this morning's elephant contest."

"What do you mean?" he demanded angrily. "I got twenty-two. You counted them yourself. And you didn't get any."

"But I did," I said, very sure of myself. "Don't you remember stopping to watch those elephants? They crossed the road in front of us. After that, they were on my side. Hey! Stop kicking me!"

"Dean!" Dad's voice was stern. "You can't count the same elephants twice. You're just trying to get Craig all riled up. And Craig, there's no excuse for kicking. Now, according to my count, Craig is the winner. No more arguments."

We pulled up at the ranger's station at the park entrance. Dad got out. "I'm going to report that dead elephant to the rangers and leave a few magazines. I suggest you all get out and walk around to stretch your legs."

Mom got out some cookies and lemonade. We found some shade under a baobab tree. But it was still hot—a dry kind of heat that burns the inside of your nose.

Dad came out a few minutes later and drank a glass of lemonade with us. "They say that's the third elephant killed in this area of the park in the past two weeks," he said. "The rangers are overworked and aren't sure if they'll catch the poachers, but they'll do their best."

We got back in the car and bumped a few hundred yards farther along the rutted road before reaching the main, tarred highway to Mombasa.

With windows wide open, we rode smoothly on to the coast. It got hotter and sweatier as we got closer. But I loved it. Soon we'd be at the beach!

Several hours later, we caught our first glimpse of the Indian Ocean as we neared the city. Mombasa itself is on an island, so we drove on a causeway, a kind of built-up bridge, and found ourselves in the crowded streets of the city. The heat closed in on us like a heavy wool blanket. We could no longer drive fast enough to create any breeze. Craig and I just wanted to get to the beach to go swimming and cool off. But Mom insisted on visiting the Mombasa fruit market first.

"We don't care about fruit," Craig begged. "Let's just get out of this town and get to the beach."

But Mom was determined. Dad found a narrow parking space near the market and we got out. Dad said, "I'll stay by the car so no one steals anything. Our suitcases look pretty tempting tied up on the roof rack."

Craig and I wanted to stay by the car, too, but Mom needed us to help carry the fruit. "This smells almost as bad as that dead elephant," Craig complained as we squeezed down narrow alleys between counters piled high with produce. I stepped in something soft. I looked down and saw that I'd smashed a rotten mango. People kept clutching at us, asking us to buy their "top quality fruits" and whispering special deals in our ears.

But Mom knew an old man in the corner

of the building who always gave her a good deal. We pushed through the crush of people until we arrived at his stall. He smiled widely and gave Craig and me each a tangerine. "Bakshish," he said, indicating the tangerines were a gift. Craig and I downed the tangerines in a hurry as we waited for Mom to buy the fruit. Then, each of us lugging a kikapu, or basket full of fruit, we pushed our way out of the market.

Just as we neared the door I felt a determined tug on my arm.

CHAPTER FOUR

The Coast

I turned to face a small, one-eyed Arab man. He smiled, showing his blackened teeth. "You want to buy some hashish? Marijuana?" he whispered. "Some ivory, maybe? What about an elephant hair bracelet?"

I tried to pull away but his fingers dug deeper into my arm. "Come to my shop, boy," he went on in a hypnotic monotone. "I got skins, all kinds of animals. You want? You come! You buy!"

I was scared. I thought this guy must be one of the black market dealers Dad had talked about. And he wouldn't let me go. I turned to ask Mom for help. But she'd disappeared down the steps outside the market. With a desperate jerk I pulled free and hurried out the door. At the bottom of the steps I turned and looked up. The little man was still smiling. "Maybe next time you buy. My shop is on the bazaar. Ask for Haji Tembo, the man who sells ivory."

I whirled around and bumped into a heavily sweating man carrying a stalk of bananas into the market. "Angalia, watch out!" he said angrily.

"Pole sana," I said, apologizing. I turned to see Mom walking back to get me.

"What's taking you so long?" she asked shortly. "We're ready to go!" Then she saw my eyes and noticed I was trembling. "What happened?"

"I'll explain in the car," I said. We got in and Dad drove down the main street of the city, trying to avoid hitting bicycles and two-wheeled mkokoteni carts filled with fruit pulled by straining men. I told my family about the man who had grabbed me in the market.

"Sounds like a black market dealer, all right," said Dad. "They must think the law can't touch them if they come up to people like that in an open place like the city market."

Dad thought about going to the police with the information but we persuaded him to drive straight to our cottage on the beach.

"You're probably right," he said. "We have no real evidence."

So we headed for the car ferry where we would cross a deep channel to Likoni on the mainland, south of Mombasa Island. Dad bought our ticket and then eased the car down the steep ramp that led to the ferry landing. The ferry was on the other side of the channel, so we would have to wait. The car was an oven. "Can I walk onto the ferry?" I asked. "I'll meet you on the other side."

Dad agreed and asked me to take Craig with me. "Be careful of the crowd of people getting off," Mom warned.

We nodded and headed down the ramp to the pedestrian entry off to the side. We could see the ferry leaving Likoni. A vendor sold green coconuts with the tops cut off and a straw inside. Craig wanted one so I bought him one. He took one sip and his eyes crossed. He spluttered the whole mouthful out. "That's terrible stuff," he said.

I laughed. "Haven't you ever tried coconut milk before?"

"No," he admitted.

"Then why did you want me to buy you one?" I asked.

"It looked nice and I'm thirsty."

I took it and tried it. The milk tasted a bit strong, but I drank it down. The ferry slowed as it approached the landing.

"I'm still thirsty," Craig complained. "How about buying me one of those?" He pointed at some homemade ice pops another vendor was selling. There were green ones and red ones, so I bought two for a shilling each. Then I gave my change to a blind beggar who sat by the side of the walkway, jingling a few copper coins together in his palm.

The ferry was unloading, so Craig and I stood to the side as hundreds of people poured off. Then we joined the crowd walking on. We climbed up some steps to the top of the open ferry. A strong ocean breeze dried our sweaty faces. From there we watched the cars driving on. We saw Mom and Dad and waved. Then we sat on a small bench and sucked our ice pops. "There's no taste!" Craig whined.

I agreed. They tasted like ice and sugar. "At least they're cold," I said. He nodded and kept sucking.

The ferry approached Likoni now. We stood up and made our way to the other end of the ferry. After it landed, we walked off the ferry and hurried up the ramp. We reached the top just as Mom and Dad drove up behind us.

"Do you two boys need a lift?" Dad asked jokingly.

We both laughed and jumped in. Now it was just a half-hour drive to our cottage on Diani Beach.

With air blowing in through the open car windows, we began to cool down. The road cut a straight line between groves of tall coconut palms. "What are those notches cut on the palm tree trunks for?" I asked.

Dad slowed down to get a better view. "Look ahead, there, and you'll have your answer," he said. I looked and saw a barefooted Kenyan man climbing up a palm tree.

"He's using the notches as footholds," I said. "So that's how they get coconuts down." As I talked we saw the man reach the top of the palm and, drawing a panga (a broad-bladed knife like a short sword), cut down some coconuts which fell to the ground.

"I'll bet I could climb a coconut tree," Craig said. "Just like climbing up some steps."

"No, Craig, it's not just like climbing up some steps," Mom said. "And I don't want you trying it."

"Aw, Mom," he said.

We had arrived at our turnoff, so we quickly forgot about climbing coconut trees. Dad slowed down on the sandy road which had jagged coral rocks jutting up like crocodile teeth. After a few minutes, we turned a corner and saw a small compound with four grass-thatched cottages. We could see the white sand beach and the ocean beyond.

"It's high tide," I said, seeing the waves breaking. "Let's go body surfing." I jumped out of the car.

"That's fine," Dad said, "*after* you help unload our things."

"Mom, Mom," Craig said excitedly. "Look, there's a palm tree growing out of that house. Right up through the roof!"

Mom laughed. "Yes, Craig, they built it that way. The tree was there first, so they built around it, leaving the palm in the veranda. And that's the house we'll be staying in. Cottage number three."

Matt's dad came over to greet us. "Welcome to the coast," he said, shaking my dad's hand. "Matt and the others have been waiting for you, Dean," he said, looking over at me.

"Where are they?" I asked.

"Down in the waves trying to body surf," he said.

I began unloading even faster. As soon as everything was in the house, I opened my suitcase and pulled out my swimsuit, which I'd packed right on top. I kicked off my shoes and changed. "I'm going swimming, Mom," I said, and ran to the beach.

I passed a young African boy about my age who was sitting in the sand. "Jambo," I said in greeting as I passed.

"Salama," he answered using the coastal greeting meaning "peace."

I saw Matt, Dave, and Jon in the water. I waved at them and charged into the waves. "Rugendo Rhinos really rally behind rare rhinos," I said as I reached the others. That's our secret club code.

"Hey, we thought you'd never get here," Matt said. "This is the highest tide we've had yet and the waves are great."

"Watch this," Jon yelled as he flattened his body and pushed forward under the crest of a wave. The wave carried him twenty-five yards before he came up spluttering, "Best ride so far today!"

Dave jumped a wave and fell off the back of it. "Too slow again," he said. "I can't seem to get the hang of this."

Matt and I spread out a bit so we wouldn't crash into each other and began riding waves. But Jon's first ride was still the best so far.

Matt looked out at some of the bigger waves. "I bet if we swam out a ways we could catch one of those waves and we'd beat Jon's record for sure."

"I don't know," I answered. "I heard the undertow is pretty strong and the water's over our heads out there."

"Yeah, but we're good swimmers," Matt said. "Let's give it a try."

I followed against my better judgment. I didn't want to admit I really wasn't a strong swimmer. We reached the bigger waves without any problem. As the first wave crested, I struggled in vain to catch it. The undertow swirled at my legs and began sucking me out. I kicked and swam as hard as I could but I was being pulled out to sea!

"Matt!" I cried out, beginning to panic. "The undertow is too strong for me. I can't swim back to shore!"

CHAPTER FIVE

Snorkeling

Matt, who had caught the wave, turned when he heard me shouting and began to swim out to help me. But I was afraid he'd be pulled out, too. "Go get help, Matt," I yelled. "I'll try to keep afloat. Just get my dad. And hurry!"

Matt nodded and swam toward shore. A surge of the riptide gripped me again and I started swimming as hard as I could, but I couldn't make any headway. I wanted to cry, but instead I prayed that God would rescue me. I could see Matt on the beach running. Jon and Dave had stopped surfing and looked out to see where I was. They seemed so far away.

I knew as a Christian that if I died I'd go to heaven. I just didn't want to drown right then. But I was getting tired of treading water.

Just then I heard a voice next to me. "I'll help you," said the African boy I'd seen on the beach. He spoke good English.

"I can't swim back to shore," I said.

"Do as I say and we'll get back to the beach," he answered. "When the ocean pulls you, just relax and let it pull. You can never win by swimming against the ocean. It's too powerful. You'll just get tired. But when a wave comes, then swim with all your strength. Rest when the ocean pulls and then swim again with the next wave."

I nodded. I had been resting when the waves pushed me toward shore. The boy pointed at a wave that was beginning to swell. "Now," he commanded. "Swim hard!"

We both swam and made progress. But after the wave passed, the undertow began pulling us back to sea. I struggled against it. The boy touched my arm. "Rest," he said.

I obeyed. We drifted out. As another wave swelled, he shouted, "Now, swim!" I did. I wasn't sure whether we'd get to shore. But at least we weren't going farther out to sea.

If only Matt would hurry and bring Dad! Slowly we got closer to shore. Then I saw Dad and some other men running down the beach. They had just reached the water when I found I could touch the sandy bottom with my feet. Now I could stand firmly against the undertow and swim in with the waves. I put my arm around the boy who had helped me.

"You saved my life," I said. "Thank you very much."

Dad splashed up and I fell sobbing into his arms. He held me tightly for a few minutes, and then we walked onto the beach and sat down.

"What happened?" Dad asked. I told him how I'd gone out too far and been caught by the undertow.

"And this boy, I don't even know his name, swam out and taught me how to use the waves to get back to shore." I turned to the boy and thanked him again and asked his name.

"My name is Salim," he said. "I live near here. My father is a fisherman. He's the one who warned me about the pull of the ocean, and how to swim with it. So the one to thank is my father."

"Well," my dad said, "your father's not here, but you are, so I want to thank *you* for saving my son's life."

Salim smiled and said, "I have to get

home. So, kwa heri, be left with blessing." With that he walked down the beach.

Dad put his arm around me and we all walked home. Matt followed slowly. I turned. "Thanks, Matt, for getting my dad."

"But it was my fault for getting you out too far," he said guiltily.

"I chose to go," I said. "But tomorrow I'll be more careful."

"And tomorrow, I'll be sure I come down with all of you boys at high tide," my dad said.

That night as we had our family devotions on the veranda, we prayed and thanked the Lord for His protection. I realized what a close call I'd had and shivered. My experience with the hippos the day before hadn't affected me as deeply. Maybe because it had happened so quickly. But today, caught in the undertow, I'd had plenty of time to think about drowning. And, even though I knew I would go to heaven, it scared me. Dad thanked the Lord for the angels he sent to watch over us. In my heart I prayed along.

I went to bed later and pulled my head under the sheet to avoid the mosquitoes. Tomorrow would be a great day. We Rhinos planned to go snorkeling near the reef at low tide.

I woke up early the next day and fixed my own breakfast. It was warm already and I could see the tide was ebbing. The reef began to appear as the water went out. I could see the pools where we'd soon be snorkeling.

I'd finished breakfast when Craig came into the kitchen and demanded that I fix him some. I put bread in the toaster and propped a rock on the handle to keep the toast down. When the toast was ready, Craig buttered it himself.

He saw my goggles and snorkel and wanted to join me. "No," I said. "We're going out to the reef and a little kid like you could get hurt. You don't even know how to swim, yet. I don't want you tagging along."

Craig started crying and ran to Mom and Dad's room. This time I won. Mom didn't want Craig on the reef without an adult watching. Dad would take him out later when he finished sleeping. That's what he liked about the coast. Not having to get up so early.

I went out to find Matt, Dave, and Jon. Dave was ready but the other two were still eating breakfast. Dave and I went on down to the ocean. Before we got to the beach I picked up a short, strong stick for poking into suspicious holes and cracks in the coral. I was always curious about what lurked in those dark holes, but I didn't like the idea of finding a moray eel with the end of my finger.

At the water's edge, I put on my reef sneakers. The coral was sharp and sea urchins were common, so we needed to protect our feet.

"While we wait for the other guys, let's try snorkeling around that mushroom-shaped coral head over there," I said to Dave, pointing at a dark shape in the water.

"How do you know that's a coral head?" Dave asked.

"I've been here before," I said.

Dave put on his mask and started to swim over. "Wait," I told him. "The glass on your mask will get all foggy unless you spit on it first and smear it around."

Dave shook his head and swam toward the coral head. The idea of spitting in his mask sounded gross to him. But I carefully followed my own advice before pulling on my mask.

Under the water I entered another world. I breathed slowly into my snorkel, hearing the deep, raspy sound as my breath came in and out. As Dave and I approached the coral head, we met hundreds of small, brilliantly colored fish. Some glowed electric blue.

Others were blinding bright orange and yellow. Some were as flat as a plate. Others looked like pencils with mouths and eyes. Some had giant eyes. Many were striped, others were spotted, all were beautiful. I turned and saw Dave signaling and pointing up. We both popped our heads out of the water to talk.

"I can't see," Dave said. "My mask is all fogged up. I guess I'd better follow your advice."

We swam above the coral head and stood up where it was flat. While Dave spit on his mask, I tightened mine a bit. Water had been leaking in under my nose.

Then we dove in again. I loved watching the fish, but I really enjoyed finding shells. So I began diving down and looking at the underside of the large coral head, the kind of place where certain cowrie shells love to hide. At first I saw nothing, but as I worked my way around the coral I found a bright orange lump. I knew it was a cowrie shell, but I was out of breath. I swam to the surface and blew the water out of my snorkel. I took another deep breath and dove down again. With my finger I touched the soft orange mantle a cowrie shell uses to cover itself. The fleshy orange mantle pulled inside, revealing a glossy bluish shell with purple spots on the edges. It was a Chinese cowrie, uncommon in this part of the Indian Ocean.

Checking to see that the shell was not sitting on eggs, I gently plucked it from the coral and put it into the white sports sock I had tucked into my swimsuit waistband. My collecting sock, I called it. I used to carry shells in a plastic bag, but it filled with water, making it heavy and difficult to carry. And when I walked on the reef and tried to dump the water out I often lost some of the shells I had collected. Then I'd heard about carrying a sock. No shells fell out and the water drained out by itself when I swam or if I stood up on the reef.

After putting the Chinese cowrie in my sock I surfaced for air. Then I began swimming toward Dave to show him my shell.

As I neared him, I saw him trying to grab something. Then I saw with horror what he was reaching for!

CHAPTER SIX

The Reef

Dave's hand was poised only a few inches from a poisonous scorpion fish. The orange-and-black striped fish was about six inches long with long, fluttering fins. Unlike other fish, scorpion fish don't swim away. They don't need to. They carry a hefty dose of poison in the fins on their backs. And Dave was just about to grab hold of this scorpion fish!

I swam as fast as I could toward him and swept my poking stick through the water and hit his arm up away from the fish. The scorpion fish darted under the coral head. Dave surfaced and, pulling out his snorkel, he spluttered, "What do you think you're doing, hitting me like that? First, you scared me. And worse, you scared that fish I was about to catch with my bare hands."

"That fish is poisonous," I said.

That stopped Dave's complaining instantly. We swam over the table-topped coral head and stood up. I explained that scorpion fish use their feathery fins and slow movements to camouflage themselves as seaweed. Then, when a fish comes too close, they inject their poison through the dorsal fins on their backs. This paralyzes their prey which they then eat.

"Would it have killed me?" Dave asked, stunned.

"Probably not," I answered. "You're a lot bigger than a little fish. But it would have stung a lot, for as long as two days, I've heard. And it would have left your hand partially paralyzed and numb for a few days."

Dave shuddered. "I'm lucky you were with me. What else do I have to watch out for on the reef?"

"The safest thing is not to touch anything you're not sure of. That's why I always carry this poking stick for touching things I don't know about," I said. "And I ask people who know—like the African fishermen."

Just then we heard Matt and Jon swimming toward us. They stood on the coral head with us to put on their masks. "Better spit on your mask first," Dave advised.

Jon and Matt both made faces at the thought. "Have it your way," Dave said. "But I've learned to follow Dean's advice. When you have your masks on, I'll show you a poisonous fish, if you promise not to touch it."

We submerged and circled the coral until we found where the scorpion fish was lurking under a flat piece of coral. Matt and Jon soon joined us and we pointed it out to them.

After we had explored the coral head some more, we decided to swim out to the main reef.

There was a deep channel where the water was well over our heads before the bottom gradually shelved into the exposed reef which looked like a crocodile's back sticking out of the ocean.

"Boy," Matt said, standing up in the shallow water and pulling off his mask, "I could hardly see anything. My mask was all fogged up. I came within inches of stabbing myself on a sea urchin before I saw what it was."

Jon complained of the same problem. Dave winked at me and said, "I told you to spit on your masks first. It's Dean's secret anti-fog solution! It really works."

Matt and Jon laughed and said they'd try it.

"But first," I said, "let's explore this stretch of reef." I was having a good time. My dad had taught me a lot about snorkeling, tropical fish, and shell collecting on other trips to the coast. Now I had a chance to teach the other Rhinos.

I bent down over a small tidal pool in the reef with live seaweed growing on the bottom. "Come here and look at this, you guys." All three came over. I showed them several raisin-size lumps on the seaweed. "Do you know what those little things are?" I asked.

"Seaweed with pimples," said Matt. "Big pimples!" We all laughed.

"Touch one," I said. Dave hesitated.

"Are you sure?" he asked. "They're not poisonous?"

To show them there was nothing to fear, I reached down and touched the soft gray lump. Within seconds the gray color disappeared, like an automatic window in a car, revealing a beautiful, pure white shell with tiny grooved lines on it. "A coffee bean cowrie," I said.

Each of the Rhinos had a great time finding other coffee bean cowries and touching the mantles and watching as the shells appeared. "This is great," Jon said. "Can we take them back?"

"Yeah," I answered, "if we each take just one. But we have to be sure the ones we take aren't females hatching eggs or there won't be any shells left for other people to see."

We walked on down the reef finding other shells, bright red starfish, sea cucumbers, brittle stars, and other sea creatures. I showed the other Rhinos how to turn over stones gently to look underneath for shells. And then to be sure to return the stones to their original position so we didn't ruin the home of all the small shells and animals living under the rock.

After we had explored the reef, Matt wanted to do some more snorkeling. "I've heard it's best on the other side of this first reef and before the second reef where those breakers are pounding."

I agreed. We decided on a point on the outer reef where we could see some large coral rocks. "We'll spread out so we can cover more territory," said Matt. "But we'll all head for those rocks."

The water between the two reefs wasn't very deep, so we could stand and rest if we needed. There were lots of coral heads and we found larger fish the farther out we swam. I saw a porcupine fish, which I lunged at with my stick. The fish inflated to triple size and its sharp spines stood out. The scared fish swam right by Jon who was so surprised he stood up and started yelling, "Dean! Dean! Did you see that fish? It looked like a balloon with quills!"

We both laughed and continued snorkeling out to the second reef. We all gathered there and told each other the things we'd seen. I showed the other guys a spider conch shell I'd picked up. I set it on its back on the reef and we watched as it stretched out its muscular foot and flipped itself over.

"I already have some of these shells in my collection and they're really hard to clean, so I'm going to leave it here. Let's help the shell find a good hiding place." So we found a place where the shell blended in with the seaweed and coral and hid it.

Just then a dugout outrigger canoe came by, an African fisherman pushing it along with a long pole. A young boy sat in the boat. I recognized him. "Salim, Salim," I called. "Jambo."

Salim motioned to the man poling the boat and said something. The canoe turned around and stopped by us. "This is my father," Salim said. We greeted the man who smiled and asked us in Swahili what we had found. We told him about the fish and then I showed him some of the shells in my collecting sock. I asked the man where I could find more shells like the Chinese cowrie.

"Not here," Salim's father said. "Shimoni. You go to Shimoni, you find shells like that. Nyingi sana," he finished, meaning there were very many shells at Shimoni.

I thanked Salim again for saving my life in the undertow and thanked his father for teaching Salim to respect the ocean. Then they poled off.

As they left, Matt asked about Shimoni. "Where is this place with all the shells?" he asked.

I told him I'd heard about Shimoni. It was about fifty miles south of where we were staying.

"Sounds like a great place to collect shells," Matt said. "We ought to go."

"Are you guys really interested?" I asked. "Maybe I can talk my dad into taking us."

Jon and Dave were eager to go, too. So I promised to ask my dad as soon as we got back to shore. *Boy, that would be great—going shell collecting at Shimoni,* I thought to myself as we snorkeled back to the beach.

CHAPTER SEVEN

Shimoni

At lunch I asked Dad about taking us to Shimoni. I told him how the fisherman had said there were lots of shells there.

Dad just looked out the window at the ocean. I was getting ready to beg, when he surprised me by saying, "Sure! I've always wanted to go to Shimoni. There's an old slave cave there, one of the biggest on the coast, and I want to see it."

"What kind of slave cave?" I asked.

"From what I've heard, it's a big hole in the ground near the harbor. Shimoni means 'in the hole' in Swahili. That's where the Arab slave traders used to keep the slaves they marched to the coast until they could get a dhow (a small, ocean-going boat) to take the slaves to the big slave market on the island of Zanzibar."

I was fascinated. "Tell me more."

"Well," Dad said, "there isn't much more to say. I've heard there are still iron shackles on the walls of the cave. I'd like to see it and then try to find some of the old people at Shimoni and see if I can get some stories of the slave trade."

"Can we go tomorrow?" I asked. "It will be a good low tide and I'm sure we'll find lots of shells. After we look at the slave cave with you, of course."

"Tomorrow will be fine," he said, reaching for the mildewed tide timetable book that came with the house. "Let's see, low tide is about eleven A.M., so if we leave here by seven, we should get there in time for you guys to do your shell collecting."

"Can I come?" begged Craig.

I was about to tell him he was too little, but Dad said, "Sure you can come. We'll have to squeeze a little in the car, but we'll all fit."

Craig was almost too excited to sleep that night. He kept asking me questions about collecting shells and what kinds of things to say to the other Rhinos. I finally told him to be quiet and go to sleep or he wouldn't wake up in time to go with us. That quieted him in a hurry.

I read a chapter from my Bible after Craig finally settled down. Then I prayed and pulled out some new comic books my mom had bought for this trip. I read them until I was sleepy and then turned out the light, hardly able to wait until the next morning.

I woke as the sun pushed itself up over the Indian Ocean. It was a beautiful sunrise. One minute I saw a glow over the ocean. The next minute the sun popped up like a round waffle out of a toaster. Then it was too bright to watch. I gently woke Craig and began collecting the things I would need for our trip to Shimoni.

After breakfast we all met at our car. Dad came out, camera bag in hand, and said, "Let's go." As we piled into the car he asked, "Did everyone bring a lunch?" Everyone nodded.

"How long will it take to get there?" I asked.

Dad told me to unfold his map and look at it. "Looks like it's about fifty miles, Dad," I said. "But the last ten miles are not on the main road."

He glanced over. "It's listed as a 'D' road for the last ten miles. Well, that part could be interesting," he said.

The paved road was only wide enough

for one car. When we met another car, both cars slowed down and drove with one wheel bouncing along the sandy edge of the roadway. Unless the oncoming vehicle was a bus. Then we had to pull off the road completely to avoid being smashed. Bus drivers believe the biggest vehicle has the right of way. Fortunately, there wasn't much traffic and we arrived at the turnoff to Shimoni in less than an hour.

But the road after that was terribly rough. It had rained recently and we had to avoid deep, miry mud swamps. The road ran through sugar plantations with the long sugar cane growing right up to the edge of the road. After a bumpy half hour, we finally rolled into Shimoni.

Dad got out and asked for directions to the cave. He came back and told us to get out of the car. "The cave is just behind those trees over there," he said.

We pushed our way through overgrown grass and weeds. Then suddenly my dad sat down. We all stopped and wondered why he'd done that. He turned and grinned. "I guess I found the entrance to the cave," he said. His feet dangled down a steep slope. We pushed back the grass and peered down into the darkness of the cave.

"It's a hole, Dad," I said.

Dad stood up and, in a crouching stance, began working his way down into the dark hole.

Shimoni, I thought to myself as I followed. *In the hole. I can imagine what those slaves must have thought when they were herded in here.*

"I'm scared," Craig wailed from the back.

"Here, I'll help you," Matt said. He seemed to like Craig. I guess that was because he didn't have a little brother of his own.

"I'm at the bottom," Dad announced. He switched on a small pocket flashlight he'd brought along. We gathered closely around him. The place was eerie. Puddles of water covered the bottom and water dripped off the roof in places.

Dad pointed out a trough in the middle of the cave. "That's where they fed the slaves, I guess," he said.

Dave was edging along the back of the cave to avoid getting his feet wet, when he hit something that clanked loudly.

"What was that?" Craig asked, gripping Matt's hand tightly.

"I don't know," Dave answered. "My back hit something hard."

Dad went over to see what it was. "Shackles," he said after examining the wall with his light. "There are iron shackles bolted into the coral wall here. I guess they were used to keep the slaves from escaping."

We all stood there, stunned by what we were seeing. It seemed hard to believe that slaves had actually been chained in this hole years before. I could almost hear the groans of the slaves and the snap of the kiboko, or hippo-hide whip, as the slavers marched their human cargo to the ships.

The air in the cave was heavy with the weight of the past. After a few minutes of silence, Dad said, "I guess we've seen enough. Seeing this place makes slavery seem so much more real."

We climbed out of the hole quietly. None of us could express what we felt. Craig was the only one who spoke. "I'll never forget that place," he said with a shudder.

Dad put his hand on Craig's shoulder. "And we *shouldn't* ever forget it," he said.

We piled into the car and Dad drove us down a winding sandy trail to the water's edge. He parked under a baobab tree.

We got out, gathered up our masks and snorkels, and walked down to the beach. "I don't have a mask," Craig complained loudly, crossing his arms. My ears started to turn red, and not from the fierce sun either.

"Dad," I pleaded, "Craig can't come out with us. Will you please keep him here?"

Dad smiled. "Sure. Craig, you stay here with me. We'll have a good time."

Craig didn't want to stay, but Dad pulled out the cooler and offered him a bottle of pop and a cookie. "What about us?" I asked.

"You can have some when you get back," Dad said. "Have a good time." Craig tried to stick his tongue out at me but his mouth was too full of cookie crumbs.

We walked down to the water and saw lots of small rocks in the shallow areas but the bottom was muddy and slimy.

"Let's go out deeper and find some coral heads," Matt said. We all followed. The farther out we went, the less we saw. We were in a channel now between Shimoni and Wasini Island and, though the water was deeper, the bottom was nothing but sand.

Matt signaled for us to swim in to where we could stand up. "Where are all the shells, Dean?" asked Jon. "We should have stayed by our cottages. At least there we saw lots of fish."

"Maybe the fisherman yesterday didn't want us to find all the shells on his stretch of reef," suggested Dave.

"I think he told us the truth," I said. "Let's swim in and find a fisherman and ask him where the best shelling is."

"Well, there's nothing out here, that's for sure," Matt said.

As we got near the shore I saw Craig walking around in knee-deep water. *I wonder why he's playing in the mud?* I thought to myself.

He saw us coming and began waving his arms excitedly. "Dean, Matt, shells! Tons of shells!" he shouted.

We gathered around him and he showed us all the small cowries he'd stuffed into his pockets. "They're under these small stones," he said. "See?" He turned one over.

"You're right," I said. "A lynx cowrie and two grooved cowries. How'd you know to look under these muddy rocks, Craig?"

"Dad told me," he answered with a satisfied smile on his face.

Dad had walked over from where he'd been sitting under a baobab tree talking to an old man. "Cowries love to live in rubble and a bit of mud like this. You guys were so eager to get out that I let you go. But this is why Shimoni is famous for shells. You don't even need to snorkel."

"Let's spread out and cover this area,"

Matt said, taking command.

"Don't be greedy," my dad warned. "Be gentle with the stones and turn them back over once you're finished looking. And when you're done, we'll look at all the shells and I'll help you decide which ones to take and we'll put the rest back."

We all agreed and went to work. I had never seen so many cowries in my life. I found lots of the more common kinds, but my prizes were a rare square-spotted cowrie and an eyed cowrie that looked like someone had painted a hundred tiny brown circles on a cream background.

After about an hour we gathered back near our car. Dad helped us identify all the shells. Then he allowed us to keep only one of each variety. The rest we took back and dropped into the ocean.

"I'm thirsty," Craig said.

"I think it's time for lunch," Dad said, breaking out the drinks. Everyone had a cold bottle of soda pop to go with his sandwich.

"Who was that old man you were talking to?" I asked Dad.

"When we stopped in the village earlier, I asked if anyone could tell me stories about the old slave trade, and that man came over here to talk to me," Dad said. "That man's father was captured as a child and marched here to Shimoni to be sold as a slave. He told me his father was so sick in the cave back there that when they herded everyone out they left him for dead. He woke up to find everyone gone. Then he climbed out on his hands and knees. A fisherman from the village found him and took him in. The fisherman and his wife raised him as their own child. That old man gave me graphic descriptions of what his father said it was like when the cave was crowded with slaves.

"Then, right before he left, he got very close to me and whispered in my ear that slavery still exists on this coast! Children are being snatched and sold as slaves in the Arabian peninsula."

"Do you think he was telling the truth?" I asked.

Dad thought for a moment. "I don't know. He seemed so earnest about it. But he is a very old man. Maybe his mind was wandering back to the past and the stories his father told him."

Just then a few raindrops started to fall. We looked up to see bruise-colored clouds covering the sun. "We'd better head for home, boys," Dad said.

We packed everything into the car

quickly, but not quickly enough. The rain pelted us before we could all climb in. Dad started driving as fast as he could, but it was like driving under a waterfall. When it rains on the coast, it really rains.

We passed through the village and were bouncing through the sugar plantations when Dad noticed how deep the water was getting on the road in front of us. "It may be too deep for our car," he said, slowing down. Before he could say anything else, the car's engine stalled.

CHAPTER EIGHT

The Coral Cave

ater must have splashed up on the distributor," Dad said. He got out of the car and was astonished to see the caramel-colored water reached almost to his knees.

"We may have to wait this rain out," he said, getting back into the car. We could see the water rising. Dad cranked the engine again but nothing happened.

"Maybe we should pray," Craig piped up from the back seat. So we all prayed, but the engine still didn't start. By now water leaked under the doors.

Matt spoke up. "It looks like there's a dry spot up ahead." Sure enough, we saw a place where the road rose slightly and the water hadn't yet covered the ground there.

"Shoes off, everyone," Dad ordered, "and

let's push the car up that rise."

We got out and splashed and slipped and shouted and finally got the car moving and up out of the deep water. Dad jumped in and put the car in gear and set the emergency brake. We were already so wet we decided to stay out and play while we waited for the rain to stop, which it did after about ten minutes. That's how rain is in the tropics. It pours so hard you feel like you should copy Noah and build an ark. And then just as suddenly it quits.

The sun came out and everything began to steam. Dad opened the hood of the car and dried the engine parts with an old rag. Soon he had the car started and we climbed in, making a mess of the back seat. The water level on the road dropped quickly as the water seeped into the sandy soil. Dad drove slowly so he wouldn't splash water on the engine again.

Finally we reached the main road and the rest of the drive home passed quickly.

At my request, Dad stopped at a petrol station near our cottages and we bought a five-liter plastic container of kerosene. When we got home I taught the other Rhinos the easiest way to clean cowrie shells. We poured kerosene into some tin cans. Then we dropped our shells in, making sure they didn't lay on their backs.

"Tomorrow," I explained, "we can take them out of the kerosene and wash the dead snail out of the shell with no bad smell. Unless you don't like the smell of kerosene, that is. But we can't forget to do it tomorrow or the shells will lose their beautiful colors."

"That was easy," Matt said. "Let's go for a walk on the beach before the tide comes all the way in." It was about the middle of the afternoon and we all thought a walk on the beach would be a good idea.

We headed north on the beach. "Let's see if we can go all the way to those coral cliffs," suggested Jon, pointing. We could see in the distance where the white sand beach gave way to black coral cliffs.

As we walked along, my feet started burning. The flaming sun had made the sand so hot it blistered my feet. But I didn't want to seem like a baby, so I didn't mention it until Dave stopped and lifted one foot up and tried to cool it down by blowing on it.

"Are your feet hot, too?" I asked.

"Sana," Dave answered, using the Swahili word for *very much.*

"Mine hurt, too," Jon said.

"Let's walk down along the water's

edge," suggested Matt. "I'll race you guys." We all ran to the water but Matt won, being the fastest and having had a head start. The water wasn't exactly cool, but at least it felt better than the burning sand.

When we neared the coral cliffs, Matt, leading the way as usual, punched his toe against a piece of exposed coral under the shallow water. We hadn't realized that where the cliffs started, the old black coral rocks stretched out into the water as well.

"Well, we can't walk any further in the water," Matt said as he nursed his big toe. "Let's go up and explore the cliffs."

We hurried across the hot sand. Then we had to cross about twenty-five yards of jagged coral to get to the cliffs. We picked our way across the coral as carefully as we could. When we reached the cliffs we walked in the shade provided by coral walls.

"Next time I'm bringing my shoes, or at least a pair of thongs," I said. Everyone agreed.

At last we reached the cliff. Small islands of sand had been caught at the base of the cliffs, making the walking soft and cool.

Some of the cliffs had small caves in them that had been carved by waves. As we stuck our head into these tiny caves we saw walls covered with limpet shells and nerites. Red-brown crabs scuttled up and down the walls, hiding in holes as we got too close.

Jon, the most adventurous Rhino, had slipped ahead. "Look at what I found," he called out. We ran to join him.

"A big cave," he said. We all looked but couldn't see any cave.

"It has a small entrance," Jon explained, getting on his knees and squeezing through the little hole. "But inside it becomes a great big cave." His voice echoed so loudly it almost scared us.

We all squirmed in. The hole wasn't that small, but it was so close to the ground we hadn't noticed it. Inside, the cave opened up into a large oval shape with a few thin, finger-shaped rooms leading to the back.

"Why isn't it dark in here?" Matt wondered aloud.

Dave had been curious as well and scanned the roof of the cave. "There's the reason," he said, pointing to some beams of light filtering down from above. "There's a hole in the top of the cave over there and light comes in through that opening."

We all sat down to rest for a while. "This is a neat cave," Matt said. "It could be our clubhouse while we're here if we need to have any Rhino meetings."

"It sort of reminds me of Shimoni," I said. "Only smaller. I wonder if it was ever used as a slave cave?"

The other Rhinos laughed. "Your imagination is too wild, Dean," Dave said. "You saw how many caves there are in these cliffs alone."

"Yeah, I guess you're right," I answered.

"Well, we'd better head for our cottages," Matt said. "The tide's rising."

"Yeah," Jon said. "I want to go body surfing."

On the way out of the cave, Jon noticed some curious, curved marks in the sand near one of the walls. "I wonder what made these tracks?" he asked.

We all gathered to look. Jon made some more observations. He's the tracker in our group. "The marks were made by something heavy, and there are two marks, almost the same, but..." he knelt down for a closer look, "they're different."

The rest of us had no idea. "Maybe a crab was pulling along a piece of driftwood," I offered.

No one thought much of my suggestion. "Well, I guess it's a mystery," Matt said.

"And we won't find the answer by staying here any longer."

We all crawled out of the entrance and headed back for our cottages. By now the sand was cooler and we ran our Rhino half-jog to get back in a hurry.

As we reached our cottages, we saw a young African boy running wildly up the beach waving his arms.

We stopped. "It's Salim!" I said. We ran over to him. "What's wrong?" I asked.

"My sister," Salim sobbed. "My sister Rehema has disappeared!"

CHAPTER NINE

Rehema

"Disappeared? When?" Matt asked. "What happened?"

Salim calmed down enough to tell us his sister had gone to fetch water in the morning and had never returned. "My mother thought she might have wandered away to play with friends. But my father and I have been searching since we returned from fishing and no one has seen Rehema."

"Are there other children missing from the village?" I asked. "Maybe your mother was right and she and some others went to play someplace where no one has seen them."

"No other children are missing," Salim said soberly. "She has simply disappeared."

"Do you think she might have gone

swimming?" asked Matt. "Dean, here, almost was drowned the other day, and..."

"No!" Salim interrupted Matt. "No! Rehema knew she was never to swim alone. That was my father's rule and Rehema always obeys."

"How old is Rehema?" I asked.

"Seven years old," Salim answered.

I realized she was the same age as Craig. And Craig didn't always obey. "Have you looked for her by the ocean?" I asked.

"No," admitted Salim. "But we've looked everywhere else."

"Then let's go down and look by the ocean," Matt ordered. We ran down to where the waves crashed onto the sand.

I felt sick to my stomach as I peered out at the waves and saw something dark bobbing up and down. "Look there!" I shouted.

"Rehema!" Salim gasped. "Oh, no!" He jumped into the water with Matt close behind. The rest of us stood and watched.

As they reached the object and grabbed it, Jon commented, "It doesn't look much like a little girl to me."

Matt and Salim headed back to shore, leaving the dark object floating on the waves. "It was only a palm branch," Matt said as he and Salim walked out of the surf.

We spent the next hour walking up and down the beach looking for some sign of Rehema. We found nothing.

Finally, as it was getting dark, we gave up. We gathered together with Salim. I put my arm on his shoulder. He seemed ready to cry. "We can't do anything more now," Matt said. "We'll help you search again tomorrow. But before we leave, I'd like us to pray. Maybe we should have done this earlier."

Salim stiffened as Matt mentioned prayer. But he stood quietly as Matt prayed for Rehema and her safe return.

Then we walked Salim back to the path that led to the fishing village. He turned to us before we parted. "Whatever happens," he said, "I want to thank you for caring about us."

At home that night I told my parents about the missing girl. Both my parents were concerned, and we prayed for Rehema and her family during our devotions.

The next morning Dad offered to walk with me down to the fishing village to see if we could do anything to help. The other Rhinos saw us going and joined us. Matt's dad came along, too.

We arrived at the village to find the

family in mourning. Loud groans and cries came out of the small house with the makuti (palm thatch) roof where Salim lived. Some policemen were talking with the fishermen. Our dads went over and joined them.

My dad came back in a few minutes. "The police assume the little girl must have drowned. They'd appreciate our help in combing the beach. They say when someone drowns, their body usually washes up on the beach the next day."

So we all walked to the beach together with a number of Kenyans from the village, Salim among them. We formed a long chain by joining hands and walked up and down the beach. The last time we'd done something like this was the year before when an older missionary lady had lost her false teeth in the waves at high tide. We'd found her teeth caught in some seaweed the next day. But on this day we found nothing.

Finally we all gave up. If Rehema had drowned, her body hadn't washed ashore. We walked back to the fishing village where we tried again to comfort Salim and his family.

Our dads talked with Salim's parents. Salim turned to us. "I know Rehema didn't drown. We haven't found her body on the beach. And I know Rehema. She's my sister.

She would not have disobeyed my father's rule about going to the ocean alone."

"But what other answer could there be for Rehema's disappearance?" Matt asked.

Salim shrugged. "I just know she didn't drown," he said stubbornly.

Jon looked thoughtful. "Where's the well where Rehema went to fetch water?" he asked.

Salim pointed with his chin. "In that direction, about half a mile," he said.

"Can you show us where it is this afternoon?" Jon asked. "I'd like to look around that place. It's the last place we know Rehema went. Maybe we can find a clue to what happened to her."

Salim agreed to lead us to the well that afternoon. But now it was too hot to do anything. We said goodbye and went back to our cottages for lunch and a chance to rest in the shade. I could feel the heat radiating from the sunburn on my nose.

After lunch I saw Salim sitting under a palm tree by the beach. *He must be anxious to go,* I thought. *I hope Jon can find something.*

I called the other Rhinos together and we followed Salim into the forested area behind our cottages. It was cool under the shade of the trees, but hundreds of bugs molested our necks and buzzed in our ears. After about fifteen minutes, we arrived at the well. It was just a hole with no protective wall around it.

"Maybe Rehema fell in," suggested Dave, peering into the well. We all tried to get a look inside the deep hole. "No, nothing," Dave said, standing up.

Jon took charge. "I want you guys to stay where you are for a few minutes while I have a look around."

Jon could track anything in the woods around Rugendo. It seemed to me he was reading a book when he explained what he'd seen in footprints.

Now he began scouring the area and the paths leading up to the well. At one point we saw him drop to his knee and reach down and touch the ground.

After about ten minutes he came back to us. "It's just as I suspected..." he started.

CHAPTER TEN

Tracking the Kidnapper

"What can you know from these footprints you've been looking at?" Salim asked desperately.

"Let me show you," Jon began, leading us near a baobab tree. "Here on the trail are the footprints of a child about Rehema's age. Of course I can't be sure it was Rehema, but this is the path leading to your village, isn't it Salim?"

Salim confirmed it was the right path. "Well, at this point near the tree," Jon went on, "the footprints stop. And they don't pick up again anywhere. Now, there are some muddled footprints right here near the base of the tree. The kind of thing you see by the edge of the well where everyone stands to get water. So I asked myself, Why are these marks here by the tree? Here's what I found."

We followed Jon behind the tree. "Can you see these sandal prints here? They're easy to identify. The sandals are made out of old rubber tires and the left foot has a distinctive tread. The other sandal has almost no tread left. And the angle of the prints here behind the tree makes me think a person was crouched here."

Matt interrupted. "So you think Rehema was taken away by force?"

Jon nodded. "That's what it looks like. And it shouldn't be too hard to follow the sandal prints. In fact, over on this side of the path you can see them and they are deeper, a sign to me the person is carrying something heavy."

"We'd better tell the police or our parents," I warned. "I'd rather not follow this person on our own."

The others thought this was good advice and we raced back to Salim's village. A policeman was still there, taking a written statement of Rehema's disappearance. Salim interrupted them telling them what we'd found.

Salim's father turned his head to listen politely, but his shoulders continued to sag. I could tell he'd given up hope of ever finding Rehema again.

The policeman laboriously wrote down

each detail of the case. Finally he put down his pencil and gave us a fierce gaze. "We have decided this young girl has drowned. Now don't bother us with this silly nonsense about kidnapping and footprints near the well." He picked up his clipboard, squinted at it, and began writing again, concentrating on each letter as he wrote it.

Salim felt awful. He started to plead, but his father gave him a long, sad look and shook his head. Matt took Salim by the arm. "Don't worry," Matt whispered as we all walked away. "We'll go back to the well and track this person down ourselves and save Rehema."

"Yeah, we'll save Rehema," Dave echoed. And we marched back to the well.

"Okay, Jon," Matt said. "Lead the way."

With Jon bent over examining the ground, we hurried along. "This person sure didn't follow any paths," Matt commented as we ran into some spiky thorn bushes.

"No," Jon answered. "I think whoever it was wanted to avoid the paths leading to the well so he wouldn't be seen carrying Rehema."

I could hardly see any tracks at all, but Jon kept on moving through the bush. We came to a rocky area. Jon stopped.

"No more tracks," he stated. We started

climbing over the rocks. But we saw no other signs anyone had passed this way. "Spread out," Jon called. "See if any of you can find a place where these tracks start up again."

We spent almost an hour looking for the trail. But we found nothing.

Matt called us all in. "Let's go sit under that tree and decide what to do next." I could tell Matt was discouraged. He rarely sat down so we could decide what to do. Usually he ran ahead, telling us what to do next.

As we sat down under the huge mango tree, Dave, always concerned with details, asked, "Salim, do you know anyone who would have carried away your sister?"

"No," Salim answered. "And that's where this whole search doesn't make sense. My father is an elder in our clan and he has no enemies. Who would do such a thing? I can think of no one."

"But the marks by the well," started Jon.

Matt spoke up. "You did a great job, Jon. But it's possible those marks meant something else. Maybe those footprints weren't Rehema's. Maybe the sandal prints we followed got heavier because the person was carrying water.

"But the sandal prints never came near the well," argued Jon.

"You didn't see them near the well," I put in. "But you have to admit that a well is a meeting place for a lot of people. The sandal prints we followed might have gone to the well but then were covered over with everyone else's footprints, including our own. And Salim doesn't know of anyone who would have snatched away his sister. The only thing that comes to my mind would be modern-day slave traders. But, of course, that's ridiculous."

"Sure it's ridiculous," Matt said. "Well, Salim, I don't know what else we can do. We can only assume, as the police are doing, that Rehema drowned. I'm really sorry."

Salim looked down at his feet. Slowly we walked back to the village. Salim saw his father talking with some of the other men of the village. He went to them and returned with the word that there would be a funeral for Rehema the next day.

"Would you like us to be with you?" asked Matt. The skin on the back of my neck crinkled. I really didn't want to attend a funeral. The way the women wailed scared me.

I could tell by the look on Salim's father's face that he didn't want us to attend. But Salim looked at us desperately, with wide eyes. "Oh, please, Father, let them come. They care deeply about us and Rehema."

To make peace, Salim's father nodded curtly. "You may attend, but bring no Bibles."

We all gave Salim a squeeze on his shoulder and promised to join him early the next day to give him some friendly support during the ceremony.

From a nearby house I heard a fluttering wail followed by deep sobbing. I prayed that God would help me not to be too scared the next day.

When we got back to the cottages we met Dave's dad. "Why are you guys so glum?" he asked.

We told him about our day and the funeral planned for the next day.

He gave Dave a hug and encouraged all of us that we were really showing the love of the Lord to Salim and his family by our actions.

"But maybe tonight's activities will help take your minds off all these problems," he finished.

"Tonight?" questioned Dave. "What's going on tonight?"

"Don't tell me you've forgotten what we have planned for tonight!" Dave's dad exclaimed.

CHAPTER ELEVEN

Beach Barbecue

"What's planned for tonight?" Dave asked.

"We're having a beach barbecue!" his dad answered. "Now we need you guys to start gathering wood for a bonfire. We're even breaking out bags of marshmallows some friends back in the States sent to us. They all mashed into one big marshmallow in the mail, but we can tear off pieces and roast them."

"Okay, Dad," Dave said without much enthusiasm. "Let's go look for some wood, guys."

None of us felt excited about the barbecue. But since the party had already been planned, we had to go along with it. We scoured the beach for driftwood. Jon collected dead palm branches. "These should burn easily for starting the bonfire," he said, defending himself as we looked questioningly at his contribution.

"Looks like we have enough wood piled up here," Matt commented. Just then his mother called for him to help carry food down to a folding table that had been set up.

We all headed back to our cottages to get ready for the barbecue. The ladies had been marinading chunks of meat all day and my mom asked me to help her spear the meat onto bamboo skewers. Craig tried to squeeze lemons Mom had cut in half to make lemonade.

Dad came in to help. "We're planning to eat by six," he said. "That way we can finish clearing up the dishes before it gets too dark. Then, when it's dark, we can roast marsh-mallows over the coals of the fire."

I helped carry the food down to the beach. Then I stood to the side with the other Rhinos. The fire burned high and gave off so much heat that none of us wanted to get close to it. Our dads took charge of cooking the meat. Maybe burning the meat would be a better description. We didn't even push to the front of the line when the food was ready. Rehema's disappearance had robbed us of our appetites.

After we finished eating we put the dishes and food into boxes, ready to carry back to the cottages. It was dark now and the fire had burned down to orange coals. Dave's dad pulled out the marshmallows and we roasted them. Good as they tasted, they still stuck in my throat.

After eating marshmallows, we sang some choruses around the dying fire. Dave's dad played lively songs on his guitar. But none of us had the spirit to sing along.

"Let's end with 'In the stars his handiwork I see,' " Dave's dad said. "Look up at the sky and see one of the most beautiful pictures of God's creation. The magnificent black blanket of the night sky punctuated by bright stars." Dads talk like that sometimes.

I could see the stars and I felt small. Maybe that was why God hadn't answered our prayers about Rehema. We were too small. I knew God cared about each one of us, but at that point I began to wonder.

Our moms gathered up the younger kids to take them to bed after the singing. Craig protested as usual, but had to go home to bed anyway.

Matt's dad came over to where we sat on a beached palm trunk. "Look," he said. "I know you guys are feeling badly about your friend's sister. But you've done about all you can do. We've prayed about it and helped Salim's family in any way we could. Tomorrow you can comfort your friend at the funeral. But for now, why don't we play a game to get your bodies moving and take your minds off the subject."

"What game?" Matt asked, looking up.

His dad scratched his chin. "Hmm. Well, how about a game of capture the flag? We dads will play against you Rhinos. What do you say?"

We all stood up slowly. "Why not?" Matt spoke for all of us. "Beats sitting here and moping."

"Okay, we'll play this right," Matt's dad said, taking a stick. "I'm going to draw a line across the beach right here. It's kind of hard to see it now, but the moon's coming up in about half an hour. For now we'll just use the starlight."

He scratched a line in the sand.

Then he called over the other dads and explained the rules. "The Rhinos will be on that side of the line. We'll be on this side. Right now, each team will take a palm branch as its flag. Tie something white on it so we'll know it's the flag." Dave ran and got a dishcloth. Jon's dad pulled a handkerchief out of his pocket. Then we each made our flags.

"Now," Matt's dad continued, "each team has twenty minutes to hide it's flag. Then we'll all meet back here and start the game."

"Any limits on how far down the beach we can go to hide our flag?" asked Matt.

"No," his dad answered, "as long as it's somewhere on the beach and not past the first row of palm trees."

"Okay, Rhinos. Let's go!" Matt ordered. We started running down the beach.

"I have an idea," Jon said. "Why don't we hide our flag up under a palm tree. Then it will be hard for them to see which branch is our flag."

But Matt was in charge. "I know, how about that cave we found yesterday in the coral cliffs? We could hide our flag there and they'd never find it or even see the entrance at night!"

"Sounds great!" I said. "And your dad said anywhere! Boy, we'll win this game for sure."

"It's a good place, all right," agreed Jon. "But if they see us just sprinting down the beach they'll know the area where we've hidden the flag. I suggest three of us veer off and pretend to hide our flag in the coconut palms right over there. Matt can then sneak down the beach, staying up close to the edge so he won't stand out against the sand. Matt can join us back at the palm trees and we'll emerge from there. That way they'll start searching for the flag in the palms. We won't even have to leave someone to defend our flag. We can all go find where they've hidden theirs!"

"Great plan, Jon!" said Matt. "Let's do it."

Jon, Dave, and I headed for the grove of palms while Matt slipped off to the side. We hid in the palms and whispered, occasionally rustling a palm branch in case one of our dads was listening. We waited for Matt to sneak back and join us.

But our quiet whispering was suddenly interrupted by the sound of Matt yelling wildly.

CHAPTER TWELVE

Back in the Cave

We couldn't understand what Matt was yelling, but his voice sounded urgent. Forgetting the game, we sprinted out of the palm grove and ran down the beach. The moon was just coming up over the Indian Ocean, creating a wide band of glimmering light on the water so that we could see Matt running toward us.

"Tusks! Tusks!" Matt yelled. "I found some tusks!"

We reached him, but we were all too winded to talk for a few seconds. I caught my breath first. "What do you mean you found some tusks?" I asked.

"What I mean is," Matt started, his hands on his knees and his shoulders hunched forward as his chest heaved for more air, "I saw some in the cave."

"Saw some what?" I questioned.

"Tusks, I tell you!" Matt said, now sitting down on the beach. "I saw two elephant tusks on the sand inside the coral cave. They were about in the same place where we'd seen those funny curved marks the other day."

Dave was skeptical. "Are you sure? Did you touch them? Maybe you just saw some shadows."

"Well, no, I didn't actually touch the tusks," Matt admitted. "As soon as I saw them I came running back to get you guys. You know, a herd of Rhinos has more courage than just one Rhino on his own." Matt was quoting one of the slogans we'd thought up for our club.

"So let's go find out if you really did see some elephant tusks," Jon said. We all sprinted down the beach.

We had tennis shoes on so our trip across the coral was less painful this time. We reached the entrance to the cave and stopped. I didn't really want to go in. I mean, if there really were tusks, someone must have put them there. And that someone scared me. Then again, if it was just some weird shadows, well, I didn't think too much of weird shadows, either. I was afraid of what the others would say about me if I mentioned my fears, so I didn't say anything. However, I did notice the others didn't rush into the cave either.

"Well, Matt," Dave said, "why don't you show us those tusks? After all, you did see them in the cave, didn't you?"

Dave's verbal jab prodded Matt onto his knees and into the cave. We followed. Standing up inside, we waited for our eyes to get used to the dimness. Some moonbeams floated in, casting funny shadows on the walls.

"I don't see any tusks," Dave commented.

"They're right over there. Come on, I'll show you," Matt said, walking toward the side of the cave. We shuffled along behind him. Crabs scuttling along the cave walls made raspy, scratching noises as their large right claws dragged when they moved. It was spooky.

"Here they are," said Matt. "See?"

Jon and I knelt down to touch the massive ivory tusks. "These sure *are* tusks," said Jon. "I wonder what they're doing here?"

"I think I know," I said. "I think this cave is the pickup point for some smugglers. My guess is someone bought these tusks from a poacher and is waiting to get them onto a boat."

Matt began to put two and two together. "Well, if someone put the tusks here to be smuggled out, that someone's going to show up to smuggle them pretty soon. And I don't want to be here when he arrives."

"Yeah, let's get out of here," I said.

"We should tell our dads and they can get the police," said Dave.

"Good idea," said Matt. "Let's go."

We began pushing each other in our haste to get out of the cave. I banged my head on a sharp piece of coral. "Ouch!" I exclaimed. "That really hurts."

"Shh!" Jon hushed. "What was that sound?"

"It was me banging my head," I answered.

"No, not you," said Jon. "I heard you. I mean that other sound. Listen!"

We all stood silently by the cave entrance. This time I heard it, too. "It sounds like a moan," I said. "And it came from that dark area over there."

Jon walked into the blackness. "Maybe we should just run and get our dads," I suggested. My heart battered my ribs. Just then something landed on my shoulder and began tickling my neck. "Something's got me!" I shouted out in fear.

The other Rhinos jumped in fright and turned to see what had happened. I frantically brushed at whatever had landed on me. It fell with a thud at Matt's feet. "It's a crab," he observed.

I felt like a fool. "Oh," I said. "I thought... well, anyway, it scared me."

Dave put his hand on my shoulder. "Don't worry," he said. "We're all a little jumpy right now."

Jon had located the source of the moaning noise. "There's a gunia (a large burlap bag) here. And there's something heavy in it."

We all gathered around as Jon untied the bag. Inside, we saw a young African girl. She looked half asleep. Her lips were swollen but she managed to talk to us. "Maji, maji, nisaidie. Niletee maji."

"She's asking us to help her and bring her some water," said Matt, translating.

"Maybe this is Salim's sister, Rehema," I said.

The girl sat up, eyes open wide. "Salim," she said. "Unamjua Salim? Salim ni ndugu yangu." Then she slumped back on the sand.

"Looks like you're right, Dean," Matt said. "She asked if we knew Salim because Salim is her brother."

"But what's she doing here?" asked Dave. "And who would be so cruel and tie her up in a sack like this?"

I looked grimly at Matt and he nodded. "I think I was right about modern-day slavers," I said. "Jon really was on the track of a child snatcher today, and now we know who he snatched. I think the smugglers meant to ship Rehema out on the boat with the ivory."

"Let's not waste any more time talking," Matt said. "Let's get her out of here before someone comes!"

Jon untied the sisal ropes that bound the girl's hands and feet. Her body was limp, so we dragged her out as best we could.

Matt went out of the entrance first to help pull the girl through. "Hurry!" he hissed once he got outside. "I think I see someone coming!"

CHAPTER THIRTEEN

Rescue

We all froze. What had Matt seen? Were the smugglers coming to collect their things? Would we be seized and sold into slavery as well? None of us dared breathe.

Then Matt's voice came in through the opening. "Sorry, guys. I think it was just the wind shaking a palm tree. I guess I'm letting my imagination get the best of me."

"Maybe so," I replied, "but let's get out of here as fast as we can." I knew this was no time to stop and have a prayer meeting, but I prayed in my heart that God would help us get away and return Rehema to her family.

Matt pulled on Rehema's arms from the outside as we tried to push her through the entrance. We finally got her out and then scrambled through after her.

"We'll have to take turns carrying her," Matt said. "Dean, you go first."

I reached down and carried Rehema in my arms. One arm went under her back and the other held her legs right behind the knees. Fear can turn a lead-legged boy into a world-class runner. I ran like I've never run before. But I soon became tired. "Matt," I gasped, "it's someone else's turn."

Matt took the next turn and we kept switching whenever we got tired. As we neared the cottages, we began shouting for our dads. "We've found Rehema!" we yelled. "Come help us carry her!" At first our dads didn't respond. My dad told me later that they thought we wanted to fool them into giving away the hiding place for their flag.

Dave's dad ran down to meet us. "What's going on?" he asked.

We sank to the sand, chests heaving. Matt spoke for all of us. "Smugglers in a cave. And we found tusks, elephant tusks, and this girl who we think is Rehema was tied up in a gunny sack...and then we thought we heard someone and we carried her and ran our fastest to get back here."

The other dads had arrived by this time. They knelt down to check on the girl. "Whoa there, Matt," his dad said. "Slow down and tell us again."

Matt slowly explained what had happened. The rest of us popped in with our own comments to fill out the story.

"Well," Dave's dad said, "let's take this girl to the village right away and see if she's really the one who's missing. Maybe they'll know what to make of this whole story."

We all ran to the village, our dads taking turns carrying Rehema. When we got there, Matt and I ran ahead to Salim's house. "Salim! Salim!" I called. "I think we found Rehema!"

Salim came out slowly, not really believing what I'd said. I turned and pointed to my dad who was carrying the girl. Salim walked closer. As he got next to her, I knew we had guessed right. Salim's arms went up and he began crying elephant-sized tears of joy. "Rehema," he said, stroking her face. "Rehema."

Rehema woke briefly, smiled, and whispered, "Salim, niletee maji."

Salim turned and shouted into the house. "Mama, Baba, Rehema yuko hapa! Mom, Dad, Rehema's here!" His parents, who had been weeping in the house, ran out. Seeing their daughter, they swept her into their arms and carried her into the house. Salim had run off to get the drink of water his sister had asked for.

The small house didn't have room for all of us. So we stood outside and waited. Dad suggested we pray. Holding hands in a circle, we prayed and thanked God for helping us to find Rehema. In the house we could hear sobs and cries of joy.

Soon Salim came out. "My sister woke up long enough to drink some water and eat a bit of ugali (stiff cornmeal porridge) and fish. Now she is resting again. My father says he will come out in a few minutes to thank you. He wants to know where you found Rehema and who had treated her so badly."

Rather than tell the story twice, we waited for Salim's father to emerge. When he did, we told him where we found Rehema and also how Jon had guessed from tracks by the well that Rehema had been carried off.

Salim's father's eyes narrowed to angry slits. "Waarabu!" he said after hearing our story, almost spitting the word out like a putrid piece of fish.

He went on to explain that some corrupt Arab traders still smuggled out things such as elephant tusks on their small ocean-going boats called dhows. Years before they had also captured young children to work as servants in Oman. But that had all stopped. Of course, he had heard a few stories that it still happened, but he had never believed it until now.

My dad spoke up. "It can't have just been the Arabs. They must have some helpers on shore who know the area and who collect the ivory and, in this case, capture young children. Is there something we can do to catch these men?"

Salim's father thought for a moment. "Yes, maybe if we can get the police to help us. These men must be with the Arabs to show them where the cave is. They have to return to the cave to load their cargo onto the dhow. But the tide will not be right for the dhow to get close to shore for another three hours."

Dave's dad volunteered to drive to the police post with Salim's father. The rest of us waited at the cottages. They arrived with two policemen within a half-hour.

"Now," said one of the policemen, "show us the cave."

We Rhinos started to lead the way down the beach. "Wait a minute," the policeman said. "These are children. We can't have them going near the cave. If the smugglers are there, the children could get hurt.

We didn't want to be left out. "Well," said Matt, "we'll stay if you insist, but we're the only ones who know where the cave is. You wouldn't want to waste time trying to find it now."

Our dads weren't too excited about our going into a dangerous area either, but they had little choice. So, with the policemen, our dads, and Salim and his father following us, we quietly ran down the beach to the cave.

Once we got to the cave, the police entered and saw the tusks and the empty gunia. They examined the rest of the cave and then made a decision.

"We will hide in the dark corners of this cave with our guns ready for when the smugglers come," said the first policeman. "Now we'd like you to go and hide on top of this coral cliff. As you can see, there is a hole in the roof of this cave. You can climb the cliffs outside and then hide near the entrance to this cave in case someone comes from that direction. It seems to us that they use the top entrance for lowering their goods into this cave. And we don't want them to drop down on us from above."

We agreed to the plan and started to move out. "We've forgotten something," I said. "If they see the gunia is empty, they may know something is wrong and escape." Seeing our palm tree flag leaning against the cave wall where Matt had left it, I went over and stuffed it into the gunia so it looked like a child was still hidden in the sack.

As we crawled out of the cave, Jon brought up the rear, tidying up the sand so it wasn't obvious that someone had entered the cave.

Outside, we found a place to scale the twelve-foot cliff. Then we hid ourselves behind some bushes near the upper entrance. We had a good view of the ocean as well, especially since the full moon was now out. We sat down to wait. And as we waited, we prayed.

About two hours later, Jon nudged me. "Look out in the water," he whispered. "Pass it on." I tapped Dave and whispered to him to look out in the water and pass it on. Soon we were all looking out to sea, watching a dark shape coming near the shore.

CHAPTER FOURTEEN

The Ambush

As the dark shape neared the shore, we could tell it was a boat, an Arab dhow with its sail furled. They anchored a little ways off the reef. We saw two men drop off the side of the boat into the water and we heard muffled voices.

"Let's warn the police the smugglers are coming," whispered Matt.

His dad answered, "We can't. The smugglers might hear us and run. We can only pray the police haven't fallen asleep."

We all nodded and prayed silently. We saw the two men from the boat reach the shore, but then lost sight of them below the lip of the cliff. We assumed they had entered the cave. We waited. But we could hear nothing. Then we saw the two men walking into the water, each carrying an elephant tusk on his shoulder.

"Dad," I said quietly. "The policemen must have fallen asleep. It's a good thing we rescued Rehema earlier. But now these men are going to escape. We can't let this happen!"

"You're right," Dad answered. "We don't have any guns and I'm sure those men on the dhow do. But if we hurry, we can wake up the police and have them ready to act when the smugglers return to get the gunia, which they probably think still has a girl in it."

We all moved silently toward the hole in the roof of the cave, keeping low to the ground. We looked down but couldn't see anything. Dave's dad had a big, black, rubber-covered flashlight. He put it down the hole, waiting until it was well inside before turning it on so he wouldn't alert the smugglers on the dhow.

To our surprise, we saw two men flat on their faces on the sandy floor of the cave. "It's the police," said Matt. "And it looks like they've been beaten up. We need to go down and help them."

"Wait!" Jon said, "What are those piles next to the wall?"

Dave's dad moved the light to reveal crumpled khaki police uniforms. We could see the silver shoulder insignias glittering in the light.

"They look like police uniforms to me," said Dave. "But why would the smugglers have pulled off the policemen's shirts after beating them up?"

"It doesn't make sense," Jon's dad said, shaking his head.

Just then we heard the crack of a rifle. We all flattened ourselves to the ground. We heard no other shots, so we cautiously looked out at the dhow. We saw four men climbing off the boat and it looked like the two in the rear had rifles pointed at the backs of the others.

"What's going on, Dad?" I asked.

"I don't know," he answered. "But we'd better lay low until we find out."

When the four men got to shore, we saw the two men with guns ordering the other two to sit down. Then they tied up the two sitting men. Looking up at the cliff, the two men with the guns called out, "It's okay. We have captured the smugglers. You can come down now."

We Rhinos let out a cheer. I looked at Matt. "I don't know how it happened, but it looks like the police have caught the smugglers."

We scrambled down the cliff and joined the shirtless policemen who were dragging out the two men from the cave. As they tied the men up, we asked them to tell us what had happened.

"We thought you'd gone to sleep," Matt said, "and then been beaten up or something."

The policemen laughed. "We decided if we arrested the first men to come ashore, we would lose the ones on the boat who would flee out to sea when their companions didn't return. And we knew we couldn't sneak up on the boat. So we waited and clubbed the first men over the heads with our rifle butts. Then we took off our police uniforms and carried out a tusk each, careful to hide our faces from the dhow as we went through the water."

"But your rifles," Jon interrupted. "How did you get your rifles out to the boat?"

"We carried our rifles on our shoulders, right under the tusks. When we had climbed on board, we dropped the tusks. I fired in the air and my friend pointed his gun at the two Arab sailors. They agreed to come quietly to shore. Now we have caught all four men, and we have the tusks and the young girl as evidence of their crimes."

"Do you know any of the men you've arrested?" Dave's dad asked.

"We don't know the Arab sailors. But these other two men have spent time in our jail before. This one is very bad. We've arrested him several times for trying to sell hashish and other drugs, as well as ivory ornaments to tourists. But we've never had solid evidence to keep him in jail."

I caught my breath and looked closely. Was he the same man who had grabbed my arm in the Mombasa fruit market? Was he Haji Tembo? Even in the moonlight I could see he was a different man. It made me sad to know there were so many people involved in the black market and smuggling.

The policeman went on. "We'll see that these men are put into jail for a long time. Imagine, trying to sell a young girl into slavery. Terrible." The two policemen jerked the four smugglers to their feet and began marching them up the beach.

Dave's dad gave the police and their captives a ride from the cottages to the police post. As he drove away, we all thanked God for the success of the operation.

Salim and his father, who had quietly observed the whole night, thanked us for our help and walked back to their village.

"Well, son," my dad said to me, "I think it's time for bed."

I yawned and nodded. Not even dive-bombing mosquitoes could keep me awake that night.

CHAPTER FIFTEEN

Packing Up

After another fun week on the sun-drenched beach, it was time to load up the car and drive back to Rugendo. I hated this part of any vacation. But I packed my things, being sure to wrap my half-cleaned shells in an airtight plastic bag so they wouldn't stink up the car. Once before, I'd packed them in a paper bag, and we'd all nearly died gagging from the smell before the trip was over.

Just before I packed my mask and snorkel, I had an idea. "Dad," I asked, "do you think it would be all right if I gave my mask and snorkel to Salim? Just to show him I love him as a friend?"

Dad thought for a second and then said, "You know, Dean, I think that would be a great idea. Come on, I'll go with you."

At Salim's village I found him just ready to go out to the reef with his father. "How is Rehema?" I asked.

"She is much better. We still can't thank you enough for returning her to us," Salim answered.

"The one to thank is God," I said. "God answered our prayers for Rehema."

Salim nodded, looking thoughtful. Dad had wandered over to talk to Salim's father.

"We're leaving today," I said, "and I wanted to give you this to show you I care about you." I handed him the mask and snorkel.

His eyes grew large. "For me?"

I smiled. "Yes, I thought you could use them when you go out to the reef with your father."

"Oh, yes! Yes!" he said. "But why are you giving them to me?"

I explained to him about how Jesus loved us enough to die for us and Jesus told his followers, the Christians, to show that love by being kind to others.

Salim nodded. "I'd like to know more about this Jesus," he said. "We are Muslims and in our religion we know about Jesus. We call him Isa. I know he was a prophet, but when you speak of him dying for our sins and coming back to life, you speak of him as God. I don't understand all this. But I'd like to hear more."

Dad walked over with Salim's father. He gave Salim one of his Christian magazines to read. "There's a story in it about another Muslim and how he became a follower of Jesus. Maybe you can read it to your father."

"Oh, yes," said Salim. "I will do that."

Dad went on, "And here's the address of an evangelist from your tribe who lives near here in the town of Kwale. If you have more questions, you can write to him and he'll visit you and talk with you about Jesus."

Salim's father nodded solemnly. "You have been true friends," he said shaking Dad's hand and then shaking mine.

"Well, we have a long journey ahead," Dad said, and we started to leave.

"Wait," said Salim. He dashed into his house. When he came out he carried a giant spider conch, a shell over a foot long with sharp fingers sticking out of it. He put it in my hands. "It is my gift to you," Salim said. "I found it myself. Kwa heri, go with blessing, and thank you for your love."

As we walked back to our car, Dad put his hand on my shoulder. "Well, Dean," he said, "this sure has been some vacation, hasn't it?"

I smiled and nodded my *head. You can say that again*. I thought.

THE RUGENDO RHINOS AND

CHAPTER ONE

Going Camping

I awoke to the clanking sound of my alarm clock. I reached over to bang the tab down to silence the noise, avoiding the broken piece of glass that covered part of the clock face. That had happened another time when I'd hammered the clock into silence, knocking the clock to the floor and breaking the glass. The fall must have jarred the innards of the clock as well, because since then the alarm had made an odd clanking noise instead of a ringing sound.

I sat up, yawned, and looked at the clock. Only the minute hand glowed in the dark. I had scraped the green stuff off the hour hand after the clock face had broken, trying to figure out why it glowed. I'd been unsuccessful in my experiment but had created a clock that was better at waking me up. I couldn't tell the exact time without turning on the light in my room. I reached over and switched on the light and looked at the clock again. Five o'clock! Why had I set the alarm so early?

Then I remembered. Today we headed for the plains on a hunting trip! When I say we, I mean the Rugendo Rhinos. I don't mean those two-horned, dinosaur-like animals that still roam Kenya's drylands. Rugendo Rhinos is the name of our club.

Matt, our leader, was in sixth grade—a year older than the rest of us. He had suggested we build a tree fort for our clubhouse. Dave was our builder. He'd designed the tree fort. Jon acted as our tracker and hunter. He loved the woods and could locate pigeons or duikers while the rest of us were trying to unhook ourselves from wait-a-bit thorns without having the fishhook-like barbs tear great hunks of flesh out of our arms or legs. I'm the fourth member of the club. My name is Dean and I'm the official Rugendo Rhino secretary.

We all live at a mission station in Kenya called Rugendo, where our parents work as missionaries. Matt's dad trains church leaders at a Bible school. Dave's dad is a builder, Jon's dad is a doctor, and my dad edits a

Christian magazine for Kenyans.

My dad gave me the idea of writing down our adventures. Once Matt had been kidnapped after we had stumbled onto a secret oathing ceremony and we'd had to rescue him. Another time, on a vacation to the Kenya coast, a Kenyan girl had been captured to be sold as a slave. But the Lord helped us save her.

But those were old stories. Today our dads were taking us on a hunting and camping safari. Men only on this trip. Dave's dad had reserved a hunting block on the Ewaso Ngiro River about sixty miles away in Maasai country.

I jumped out of bed and began rushing around to get ready. I pulled on my favorite pair of cut-off shorts, being sure to put my red Swiss army knife in my pocket.

I found Dad in the kitchen with a mug of coffee in his hand. He'd already packed several boxes of food and stacked our tent and two sleeping bags by the door. I sat down to eat a bowl of cereal. Just then a sleepy voice complained, "I still want to go with you." It was my younger brother, Craig. Dad picked him up and explained again that he was too young for this trip. But soon he'd be old enough. Craig grumped his way back to bed.

"We decided to take two Land Rovers," Dad said. "That way if one breaks down or gets stuck, we can get help with the other. Besides, it would have been crowded in just one vehicle."

I nodded. Just then a car's lights shone in our window. I jumped up. "It's Matt and his dad," I announced. We carried our things out and packed them in the Land Rover. Then we piled in and drove to Dave's house to meet the others.

Matt and I sat on the hard metal benches that lined the rear of the "Landy," as we called it for short. When we hit a speed bump, Matt and I flew off the benches, banged our heads, and then bruised our rears on the corner of the benches. Matt moaned in agony about the hard seats. His dad told us to unroll a couple of sleeping bags as padding. We were doing that as we pulled into the driveway to Dave's house, where his dad's Land Rover stood ready to go.

"Dad, can all us Rhinos ride in the back of our Landy?" Matt asked. "We're just getting it padded and comfortable."

"Sounds all right to me," his dad said. "But we'll need to transfer some of this camping gear to the other car."

We jumped out and helped with the packing. Then Dave got in with us and we drove to pick up Jon and his dad.

The sunlight was just starting to spread across the valley in front of us as we left Rugendo. The highland morning chill disappeared quickly. It would be a hot day. Within half an hour we were on the floor of the great Rift Valley. We had another thirty miles to drive before reaching the other side. Passing two extinct volcanoes, Mt. Longonot to the right and Mt. Suswa to the left, our vehicles plowed through the thick, gray volcanic dust.

Dust filled the back of the Landy and we started coughing. "I have an idea," Dave said, pulling out a red bandanna. He tied it around his face like a masked bandit from one of my cowboy comic books. "Hey, it works great," he said, his voice muffled. None of the rest of us had bandannas, but we followed his example by covering our faces with the front of our shirts, and it became bearable.

Matt tried to get us to sing some songs, but we all felt too uncomfortable. Instead we hunkered down and buried our heads. After what seemed an eternity, Matt's dad said, "There's Narok up ahead. We'll stop and fill up the gas tank and buy a soda to drink. That dust made me kind of thirsty. How about you guys?"

We all nodded and jumped out of the Landy as soon as it had stopped by the gas pump. As the attendant pumped the gas with the hand-operated lever, we all walked into Haji Issa's store to buy sodas. The sodas were warm, but at least they were wet.

As we drank, my dad said, "Well, boys, we're only about half an hour away from our campsite. Think you'll survive the rest of the journey?"

We all started talking at once about what animal we wanted them to shoot for supper.

Leaving Narok, we bounced down the road for another eight miles before coming to the Ranger Post where we checked in to our hunting block. The game rangers looked at our dads' licenses and checked to see that they'd made proper reservations. My dad then passed out some copies of the Christian magazine he edits. The rangers immediately began reading and hardly noticed as we drove past the barrier and into the hunting area.

Dave's dad knew of a nice camping spot under some big yellow fever trees at a curve in the river, so he led the way in his Land

Rover. After driving five miles on a dirt track, we arrived. We all wanted to go hunting right away. Jon got on his knees and looked at foot prints and told everyone what kind of animals had been down to the river the night before. "Here's impala and kongoni and even a giraffe."

"First things first," my dad said. "We need to set up camp and then we'll decide about our first hunting drive."

We started carrying out the gear and helping set up camp.

"One job you boys can do is to dig a hole for our bathroom," Jon's dad said. He'd brought along a small bathroom tent that even had a stool. But someone needed to dig a small pit. He handed Jon a jembe, or African hoe. Pointing out a spot a short distance from the main camp, he sent us to dig.

The nose-blistering sun beat down so viciously we decided to take five-minute turns. Jon dug first. Then Matt. Then it was my turn. But I hadn't hit the hard dirt more than three times when I heard a soft blowing sound, like the hiss of a bike tire that's hit a thorn. With the jembe in my hands, my eyes turned to where I'd heard the noise. What I saw under the bush made my blood freeze, despite the heat.

CHAPTER TWO

Snake!

Under a bush no more than six feet away, a snake as thick and as long as a baseball bat moved slowly toward me.

"Snake!" I yelled. Or tried to. Fear tightened my throat and the word merely croaked out. But the other Rhinos understood me, and they started to clear out. With my eyes fixed on the slow-moving snake, I stepped backward so I could turn and run. But I stepped into the hole we'd been digging and fell on my back.

I don't remember praying, but I know in my heart that I screamed out for God to save me. I scrambled to my feet still clutching the jembe. By now the snake had almost reached me. In desperation I swung the jembe down as hard as I could. God must have timed my swing because I cut the snake clean in two.

Then I dropped the jembe and ran to join the others.

By now the shouting had aroused our dads and they ran to see what was happening. When I saw my dad, I ran into his arms and began to cry. Not out of fear, but from a crazy feeling of relief that I was alive and the snake was dead.

"I killed it," I sobbed. "I killed that snake with the jembe."

My dad held me for a few minutes. Then we all walked over to inspect the dead snake.

As we neared the spot, Matt jumped back. "It's not dead!" he shouted. "I can see it wiggling around!" His dad reassured him that dead snakes usually moved around for a while.

We gathered around the snake. Jon's dad took the jembe and picked up the snake's head with it. "Puff adder," he said after a closer look. "They're deadly poisonous, so we can thank the Lord it didn't bite any of you boys—*and* for your bravery, Dean."

I shivered to think of what had happened. "I didn't feel very brave. I just whacked the snake in terror. I think I'll have bad dreams about it. I can still see it in my mind. It seemed like it moved in slow motion."

"That may be because puff adders do

move in slow motion," my dad said, putting his hand on my shoulder. "God gave puff adders an extra dose of poison to make up for how slowly they move. Usually they wait and ambush small rodents. I thank the Lord it wasn't a black mamba. That's one of the deadliest snakes in the world, as well as the fastest."

"Look how its mottled brown and yellow skin looks so much like the ground," said Jon, pushing on the dead snake's body. The snake gave one last convulsive twitch and we all jumped away.

"I think we'd better dig our hole somewhere else," Dave's dad said. "Most snakes live in pairs, and this snake's mate may come here and I don't want to have a puff adder catch me with my pants down." We all laughed at his joke, a bit surprised that a dad could talk like that.

They gave me the honor of having the first cut in skinning the snake. I drew my red Swiss army knife out of my pocket and made a long cut down the soft yellow underside of the snake. Then with our dads helping, we skinned the snake. We dropped the carcass and the head into the hole we'd dug and piled dirt on it.

Then Matt's dad warned us not to hang

around that area too much and he went to dig another hole for our bathroom tent on the other side of the camp.

We carried the snake skin back to camp and poured salt on the inner side to cure it. Then we stretched it out to dry, pegging it on a fallen tree near camp.

"We can hang it on the wall of our tree fort when we get back to Rugendo," I said. Everyone was excited to have a real snake-skin in our clubhouse.

"You boys hungry?" called Dave's dad. We all said we were. "Then run around and collect some firewood and we'll cook up some lunch."

We gathered branches of a few old acacia trees that had toppled over near the river. We had to be careful to avoid the two-inch thorns on the branches. But soon we'd collected enough for the fire. Dave's dad had gathered some big stones and placed them in a small circle. We built the fire inside the circle. As the fire burned down to orange coals, Dave's dad set a big smoke-blackened pot on the coals. "How does chili sound?" he asked. Our stomachs began rumbling as the chili in the bowl began bubbling. Dave's dad handed Dave a big wooden spoon with instructions to keep stirring the chili so it wouldn't burn.

Then he made up some thick biscuit dough. "Cut yourselves a long, green stick each and you can have biscuits to go with the chili," he said.

Within minutes we came back with the sticks. Jon had cut an extra stick for Dave, who continued to stir the chili. We put globs of dough on the end of the sticks and then baked the biscuits by placing them close to the coals. Some got burned on the edges and remained doughy in the middle. But they turned out pretty good.

By now camp was set up and we gathered to eat. My dad prayed, and in addition to thanking the Lord for the food, he gave a special prayer of thanks for watching over us when the puff adder had come. I said amen to that!

Then we filled our stomachs with the chili, made extra hot with the chili peppers Dave's mom had bought at the Indian bazaar in Nairobi.

After we'd eaten, Matt asked when we could go hunting. "Let's go right now," he said. Our dads told us we'd head out of camp on our first hunting drive at about four P.M. "Right now most of the animals are hidden away in thickets to avoid the heat," he said. "But later in the afternoon they come out to feed. We'll go out then and shoot something to eat for supper."

"Let's shoot a Tommy," Matt pleaded, referring to a Thomson's gazelle.

"No, a warthog," interrupted Jon.

Matt's dad scratched his head. "Well, we have licenses for both, and both make nice juicy steaks. So let's toss a coin for it." He pulled out a silver one shilling piece and flipped it.

Jon called tails and he won. I should have told Matt that Kenya shillings almost always come up tails. The engraved head of the president is so large that it makes the head side much heavier so a coin toss usually comes up tails.

"A warthog it is," Matt's dad said, picking up his shilling from the ground and blowing off the dust.

It would be two more hours until we left. Our dads had pulled up some camp chairs under the shade of the tree and were dealing a Rook game. We Rhinos decided to go exploring on the banks of the river.

CHAPTER THREE

Skeezix

Matt led the way to the river bank. After all, he was our club captain. The river snaked along, cutting its way through the soil and leaving eight-foot banks in places, so we had to peer over to see the water, brown like the color of chocolate milk.

"Let's see if we can cross the river," Matt announced after we'd hiked for a while.

"I'm not sure," I warned. "The river's not that far across but it seems pretty deep. And who knows what lives under that water? Maybe hippos, crocodiles, even snakes!"

"Don't be so weak-kneed, Dean," Jon retorted. "Let's go across."

"Actually," Dave said, "I saw a place back around the bend where we could cross without going into the water."

"What do you mean?" Matt asked.

"Back there, two trees fell across the river. It won't be easy, but I think we can go across on those trees."

"Well, let's get going," Matt commanded. "You lead the way, Dave."

Dave had a big smile on his face as he led us tramping back down the river bank. "Here's the place," he said, pointing out where two of the many yellow fever trees that lined the river bank had fallen over. "The trees should be strong enough to hold our combined weight. And those big branches that reach down below the surface seem to indicate the trunks will be stable and won't twist or fall in." We always listened to Dave's calculations. He always thought things through.

"Who wants to go across first?" asked Matt. Jon volunteered right away. He scrambled across the fallen trees as nimbly as one of the vervet monkeys that chittered in the trees around us.

"It's easy," he yelled back to us when he'd reached the other side. "And over here I see some small animal tracks. Looks like they're from a dik-dik. I'm going to follow them."

"Wait for us," said Matt teetering his way across the trees. That's the way Jon was.

Never afraid of anything and always going into any new adventure full speed ahead. Dave followed, taking careful, measured steps as if he'd calculated exactly where to set each foot.

Now it was my turn. How could I tell the other Rhinos I was scared to death? Jon and Matt were already tracking. Dave stopped to wait for me. "Come on, Dean," he encouraged. "It's not that hard. Just don't look down."

I wanted to go back to camp. But I couldn't think of any good excuse to leave. So, taking a deep breath, I stepped onto the log. I struggled to keep my balance and did pretty well.

Suddenly Jon's voice ripped through the air. "Hey, guys, come over here! Look what I found."

I looked up, startled. I lost my balance and began to wobble back and forth. Dave said later my eyes looked double their normal size. I don't know about that. All I remember is desperately trying to keep from falling.

When I knew I couldn't regain my balance, I threw myself forward, grasping onto the tree trunk with my arms. I held on as tightly as I could, sprawled flat out on the log, my chest heaving.

"Dean! Dean, are you okay?" Dave asked. He began crawling out to help me. "Try to crawl across," he said when he got closer.

My arms felt like they were stuck to the log. I didn't want to let go. "Just release one arm first," Dave said, "and try to crawl across."

Just then Matt's head popped up out of the bushes. "You guys should see what Jon found in... What's going on? Are you two all right?"

Dave turned and told him how Jon's yelling had made me lose my concentration and I'd almost fallen in. As the others watched, I forced myself to let go of the log and crawl across. It may have seemed baby-ish, but I made it.

On the other side, I checked my arms for cuts and scratches. "I'll need to put something on these cuts when we get back to camp to keep them from becoming infected," I said.

"Jon's dad can do that," Matt responded. "Boy, I'm glad you're safe. Come see what Jon discovered."

I was still shaking. "You'll never believe this," Matt said.

We followed Matt and soon heard some loud buzzing. Bloated metallic blue flies flew around, thick as volcanic dust. We came from behind a bush to find Jon holding something brown in his arms. The flies swarmed around something squishy on the ground.

Jon said, "Somebody set a wire snare here and caught a mother dik-dik. It's pretty gross. The wire cut through her neck. But look what I found snuggled right next to the dead dik-dik. A little baby dik-dik."

We all looked at the small antelope in Jon's arms. It was the size of a small rabbit.

"Let's take him back to camp and show our dads. Maybe they'll let us keep him for a pet," said Matt.

We were all excited to get back with the baby dik-dik. I said, "Its not a rhino, but maybe we could have him for our club mascot."

The other guys liked my idea. We headed back for camp. At the log crossing, Jon went over first with the dik-dik in his arms. I went next, and even though the others might have laughed, I crawled across to be sure I didn't fall in.

Back at camp we called our dads. "Look what we found," Jon said.

My dad was the first to reach us. He took the baby dik-dik from Jon and said, "Well, looks like you boys have found a little Skeezix."

"What's a skeezawhatever you said?" asked Dave. "We thought it was a baby dik-dik."

My dad laughed. "It *is* a baby dik-dik. Skeezix was the name of a comic character when I was a kid. The name kind of tickles my tongue and I call any abandoned baby animal Skeezix until we find a better name."

"Hey, I like Skeezix," Matt said.

I was embarrassed by my dad's story until Matt said he liked the name. So we called our new dik-dik Skeezix.

We spent the next hour fussing over Skeezix, trying to get him to drink some powdered milk we'd mixed up. He didn't take to it very well and we didn't have a proper bottle to feed him.

After several attempts to pour the milk down Skeezix's throat, we had more milk on us than in his stomach.

Dave rigged up a cardboard box we'd brought food in while the rest of us gathered dry elephant grass to make a little bed. Then we picked some green grass from the river bank, hoping Skeezix might munch on that.

"Time to go shoot something for supper," Dave's dad called. "Are you boys ready to go?"

"Yes," Matt shouted, answering for all of us. Then, turning back to the box that held our new mascot, he stroked the little animal. "Goodbye, boy," he said. "We're going to do a little hunting, but we'll be back."

We all made our farewells, running our hands over Skeezix's silky back. Then we ran to the Land Rover. The day was cooling off and animals were coming out to feed.

And here's the best part: We Rhinos got to ride on the roof of the Landy as game spotters!

CHAPTER FOUR

Hunting for Dinner

We bounced up and down on top of the Landy as we drove around looking for an animal for supper. We knew we were after a warthog, but when you're hunting, you sometimes have to shoot what you find. So we kept alert, looking for anything we could eat.

We spotted some zebra grazing in a patch of leleshwa bushes. Even though we had eaten zebra before, it wasn't our choice of meat for supper. So we kept on looking.

I saw some Grant's gazelle and lifted my hand to pound on the roof, the signal to our dads that we'd seen something worth shooting. But Jon stopped me. "You can't be sure about a Grant's meat," he said. "Sometimes it's too full of worms to eat, especially around this river area. If they shot one and it was wormy, we wouldn't get supper. We'd better pick an animal we're sure of."

The Land Rover jerked off the dirt path and jolted over the grass-covered plains. "Hold on tightly," Matt said. "This area is full of small anthills and that means there will be ant bear (aardvark) holes. We won't be able to see an ant bear hole until the Landy hits it. And if it hits one, we're in for one mighty bump!" I tightened my grip on the spare tire I sat on to cushion the bumps.

"I wonder why our dads came over this way?" asked Dave. "It seems pretty bumpy to me."

"I think I know," said Jon. Jon knew almost everything a kid could possibly know about animals, even though he'd lived in Kenya the shortest time of any of us in our club. It seemed he was born to live in the bush.

"Warthogs like to live in abandoned ant bear holes," he explained. "I'll bet this plain is full of warthogs."

We all began looking for straight black sticks moving through the yellow elephant grass. The straight black sticks were actually warthog tails, held erect whenever the animals would run through the grass. In grass this high, it would be the only part of the pig we could see.

Not surprisingly, Jon saw them first. Pointing at two big fever trees with one hand, he slapped sharply on the Land Rover cab's top with the other. We looked where he pointed. Sure enough, we could see three warthog tails moving through the grass. The Land Rover slowed to a stop and Jon leaned forward and showed our dads where he'd seen the three warthogs.

Just then the pigs moved into some shorter grass near the trees and stopped running. Kneeling down, they started digging up some roots with their curved upper tusks. I wanted to laugh, the animals looked so funny. My dad always said warthogs prayed as they ate. But this was the first time I'd actually seen what he meant.

Dave's dad, who was driving, headed the Landy on a slow course parallel to the trees. The warthogs stopped eating and looked at us. But Dave's dad kept the car moving in an even rhythm without getting any closer. When we were about even with the pigs, Jon's dad quietly dropped out of the car door opposite the animals and slithered behind some tufts of grass. The warthogs kept watching our Land Rover as it slowly moved away. Satisfied we'd left them alone, the pigs went back to feeding.

Looking back from our vantage point on the roof, we could just make out Jon's dad, edging his way closer to get a clear shot. We quietly discussed which one he'd try to shoot. "Probably the big male," Matt said. "Do you see the size of those tusks? They curve so far they almost make a complete circle!"

"And his mane," I pointed out. "It's so long the hair flops over from his back and almost reaches his stomach."

Suddenly a terrific crack filled the air. The next few seconds blur together in my mind. The big pig rolled over once in a cloud of dust and then jumped to his feet and sprinted through the grass, his stick-like tail the only part of him we could see. The other two pigs crashed away as well. Jon's dad leaped up and shouted, "Let's follow him. I must have only winged him." Dave's dad stepped on the gas and turned back, picking up Jon's dad, and then hit high gear slashing through the grass in pursuit of the wounded warthog.

We could just see the tail now as it zigzagged and slowed. "Your dad got a good piece of him," Dave said to Jon. But Jon was disappointed that his dad hadn't dropped the pig with one shot. We always bragged about what good hunters our dads were. And for Jon, the best bushman in the club, it was even more embarrassing that his dad had only wounded a big fat pig. He could only mumble something about how his dad should have squeezed the trigger instead of jerking it.

The pig's tail disappeared. "The warthog must have gone down," Jon announced. He had a hopeful look on his face. Maybe the pig would die from one bullet after all.

The next thing I remember was the Land Rover slamming to a complete stop. The spare tire I was gripping lifted up with the force of the blow and I found myself flying in the air over the hood of the Land Rover and then landing heavily in the grass.

I vaguely remember my dad kneeling down next to me, asking if I was all right. I nodded. But I had a stabbing pain in my side, and I couldn't make myself move. Jon's dad, a doctor, did a quick examination before allowing my dad to pick me up. All my bones were still intact, but I winced when he touched my side.

"It seems you've probably bruised a kidney," he said. "We'll have to watch that. But your back and neck are okay and you have no broken bones."

My dad lifted me up gently and told me how Dave's dad had driven smack into an ant hill camouflaged by bushes. It had stopped us like a cement wall. The other guys had been holding on to the roof rack, so they hadn't fallen off. I had been grasping the spare tire, which I thought was tied securely to the roof rack. "I guess it makes a difference what you're holding on to," I said.

"You're right," my dad said. "You know, that would make a good sermon illustration about how having faith doesn't help if the object of our faith isn't God. You had a firm grip on the tire, but it let you down because it wasn't anchored to the roof. Many people trust in things or money or other gods to save them. They believe and have sincere faith, just as you held tightly to your tire. But their faith is in the wrong thing."

"Enough, Dad," I interrupted. "It's not time for a sermon."

He smiled and said, "You're right. I'm sorry."

Once Jon's dad said I wasn't badly hurt, the others rushed through the grass to find the warthog. Jon had marked the spot where he'd last seen the tail and found the dead pig.

He called everyone over with pride.

"Here it is, and my dad hit him with a perfect shot in the heart." I wanted to see the pig, so my dad helped me up and I limped to join the others. Sure enough, it was a perfect heart shot.

"How'd he run so far?" Matt asked. The men shrugged. "Sometimes animals do that," Jon's dad said. "Maybe it's the nervous system working. Or it may take an animal a few minutes to realize it's dead. But whatever it is, we have our supper."

I watched as the others began to cut up the warthog into steaks for supper. Jon looked up at his dad, no longer embarrassed. "That was a great shot, dad! Can I keep the tusks?"

Jon's dad put an arm on his shoulder and squeezed it. "You sure can," he said.

Then we packed the meat into the back of the Land Rover and headed for camp and warthog steaks roasted over the campfire.

"Something's wrong here..." Matt said as we drove into camp.

CHAPTER FIVE

Robbery

We all looked in disbelief. Tent flaps waved in the breeze. The cook tent had collapsed on its poles and empty cardboard boxes were scattered around. The Land Rover jerked to a stop and we all jumped out.

"Our food has been ransacked," my dad said. "There's only a few boxes of cereal left and they've been partially dumped out."

"Our sleeping bags are gone, too," Jon said after inspecting our tent.

We searched the camp, everyone reporting on our losses. Then we came back to the Land Rover. Matt's dad looked at all of us seriously. "It appears we've been cleaned out, boys," he said. "We can thank the Lord our money and licenses and important things like that were in the car with us. Even though we all feel pretty badly about losing our stuff, let's stop and pray and thank God we're safe and we have money to get home, and they didn't damage the second Land Rover we left here."

It sounded strange to me to stop and thank God when a robbery had just happened. But our dads started praying. As we stood with our eyes closed, listening to the prayers, we began to appreciate how good God was. My dad prayed about creation and all the things that surrounded us to remind us of God's greatness. Then he prayed about how sin in the world caused problems such as robberies. When we finished praying, our stuff was still gone, but I felt better.

"We do have our warthog for supper," Dave's dad said. "But we might have to cut our trip short. It's going to be pretty uncomfortable sleeping with no sleeping bags. You boys get some more wood and we'll have nyama choma (roast meat) for supper."

We scattered to get some wood. I couldn't go as fast as the others because my side still ached from falling off the Land Rover. But I picked up small twigs to get the fire started. As I hobbled along, I found one of our cardboard boxes. I kicked it and some grass flew out of it. Grass! This box had been the one with Skeezix.

"Skeezix!" I shouted. "Oh, no! We've lost

Skeezix!" The others came running. In our confusion over the robbery, none of us had remembered our new pet dik-dik.

Matt kicked the box over again. "We've lost our new club mascot," he said. "We'd better do something to get him back."

At the campfire we cut pieces of meat and put them on green sticks and held them over the coals. The meat was tender and juicy. Even without salt, which had been stolen along with everything else, we wolfed down the meat. After supper we sat around the campfire and discussed what we would do. None of us boys wanted to go home the next day. We decided to see how we slept that night. If we managed okay, we would think about staying the full four days. Our dads would drive to the Ranger Post in the morning to report the robbery and see if they could buy some food supplies at one of the dukas or shops there.

We then began to sing songs by the campfire. Jon's dad had a deep bass voice. First we sang some cowboy songs my dad had taught us. Songs like "Tumbling Tumbleweeds" and "Cool Water." Then we drifted into some Christian choruses.

"Lie on your backs for the next song," Jon's dad said. He sang out in his rich voice, "In the stars his handiwork I see. On the wind he speaks with majesty..." Shivers ran up my spine as I sang about God creating the stars while looking up at the thick, white blanket of stars that made up the Milky Way. I could also see the Southern Cross lighting up the horizon. The sky was a glut of stars. After that song, our problems seemed pretty small.

We paused and heard a Whoo-oo-up! in the distance. "Hyenas," Jon said. "I wonder if they're eating what's left of our warthog."

"Could be," his dad said.

We felt sleepy, so we began to get ready for bed. Dave's dad got the emergency flashlights out of the Land Rovers, so we could have a light in each tent. Soon he called out, "Look what I found!" He pulled out the sleeping bags we'd used that morning to protect our rear ends from the hard Land Rover benches. "There's not enough for one apiece, but we can sleep close together and cover up with these unzipped and spread out."

We praised the Lord for those sleeping bags because it can get pretty cold on the plains, even in Africa.

The four of us Rhinos bedded down in our tent under one sleeping bag. We had trouble going to sleep right away. Every move put an elbow into someone's gut or clunked a knee into someone's thigh. "I can't sleep," Matt declared. "Dean, you feel like you're made entirely out of elbows, ankles, and knees. While we're awake, let's decide what to do about our missing dik-dik."

I didn't have any idea what we could do. I'd given Skeezix up as lost or dead. Another whoop from a hyena convinced me that even if the robbers hadn't taken the little guy, he would make a quick snack for one of those steel-jawed hyenas.

But as I thought about our Skeezix being chopped into two pieces in one bite, Dave began talking about looking for footprints the next morning. Jon latched on to that idea. "Yeah, if there aren't any dik-dik tracks, then we know he was carried away. We can then search for footprints and find where the robbers took our mascot. And if there are dik-dik prints, we can follow them. Skeezix is too young to have run far. We should have thought of that tonight!"

"It was too late, tonight," Matt said. "It was already getting dark when we got home."

I didn't want to be a wet blanket on the next day's expedition. But I had some concerns. "What if the robbers are armed?" I asked.

"Oh, we wouldn't attack them," Matt said. "We'd just find them and then figure a way to sneak in and get Skeezix back. Anyway, like Jon said, we may discover that Skeezix just ran away."

"Well, I think we should ask our dads about it," I went on. Normally I wasn't scared about tracking through the bush alone. But this time, I was a bit frightened.

"No way," Matt said. "They'd veto it right off and we'd never know what happened to Skeezix. I say we let our dads go off and report this robbery and get supplies. Then we start scouting around, using Jon's tracking skills to find out what happened. We can leave a note behind explaining where we've gone, if that will make you feel better."

It didn't make me feel better. But I knew there was no use arguing with Matt. I'd tried before and lost. That's why he was club captain and I was secretary.

Another hyena whooped, very close this time. "That sounded like it was right next to the camp," I said.

"Oh, go to sleep, Dean," Matt said. "You're an old worry wart."

Just then we heard a shout and the crack of a rifle shot.

CHAPTER SIX

Psalm 91

What was that?" Matt asked, jerking up and pulling the sleeping bag off of all of us. Scrambling to find our flashlight, we unzipped our tent and peered outside.

"What's going on Dad?" I called. We got no answer. "Dad?" I called again, fearfully. "Dad, are you all right?"

"Where's our dads?" asked Matt, boldly walking toward their tent. The flap was open and he shone the flashlight inside. "No one here," he said. We bunched closely behind him. None of the others would admit their fear, but I could tell from the way we huddled together that I wasn't the only one trembling.

Jon, always the puzzle solver, examined the inside of our dads' tent. "There's no flashlight," he commented. "They must have taken the time to pick it up before going out. There's no sign of a struggle. I'm sure they must be okay."

His observations helped calm our growing panic, but the question remained: Where had they gone?

Then we heard a voice. "Did you get him?"

"I think so," another voice answered. "But I can't find him."

"Dad! Dad!" called Matt, who had the loudest voice in our group. "Where are you? What's going on? Are you all right?"

"You boys get back in your tent right away," Matt's dad answered. "We're having a snake hunt."

We scampered back into our tent and zipped it shut. "We don't know exactly what's happening," said Matt, "but I think we should pray for our dads right now." He led in a short prayer for safety.

Then Dave reached for his Bible. "Yesterday I read the most amazing verse. Let me show it to you." He turned to Psalm 91. "This psalm talks about how God is the one we turn to for safety, like Matt just prayed. But listen to verse 13."

He began reading, "You will tread upon

the lion and the cobra; you will trample the great lion and the serpent."

I looked over his shoulder. "And look what it says in verses 9 and 10. 'If you make the Most High your dwelling—even the LORD, who is my refuge—then no harm will befall you, no disaster will come near your tent.' "

Jon was following along as I read. "You have to include verse 11, too," he said. "It says, 'For he will command his angels concerning you to guard you in all your ways.' "

"Wow, God has made some specific promises for safety if we turn to him," said Matt. "He won't let disaster come near our tent, he'll send his angels to guard us and will save us even if we step on a snake. And dad said they were having a snake hunt. Let's pray again, asking God to keep these promises. Especially about the snake."

We prayed again, thanking God that he'd promised to keep us safe and asking that God's angels would protect our dads as they hunted for a snake.

As we finished, we heard footsteps coming toward our tent.

"Come on out, boys. Everything's all right," Matt's dad called. We unzipped our tent to see our dads standing there. My dad held a headless snake.

"What happened?" I asked, stepping out. "We heard a shot and then couldn't find any of you." I wanted to hug my dad, but the dead snake dangling in his hand kept me away.

"I was going to use the bathroom," Dave's dad began, "when I heard a hissing sound at my feet and then something banged hard against my boot. I jumped back, too startled even to shout. I didn't have the flashlight, but the stars gave enough light for me to make out a snake latched on to the side of my boot. I kicked and he flew off into the bushes. I realized its bite hadn't reached my foot. But I didn't want to leave an angry snake in the bush by our camp. So I went and got the others and we went snake hunting."

"Two of us took .22 rifles," said Jon's dad. "The other two took pangas [large, sword-like knives for cutting bush] and we went on a snake hunt. I thought I saw the snake and I shot, but I missed."

"Not surprising," Jon said, defending his dad. "It's pretty hard to hit a snake at night with a .22."

"Who finally killed the snake?" I asked. "Did you, Dad?"

He smiled. "Yes, I did, Dean. We were making wide circles in the area where the snake had been thrown at first. I carried the flashlight and the beam caught a flicker of motion. I swung the panga and cut the snake's head from its body."

Jon stepped closer to examine the snake. "It's another puff adder. Do you think this is the mate of the one we killed this morning?"

His dad nodded. "It seems likely."

Dave had moved next to his dad. "We prayed God would protect you with his angels like we read in Psalm 91. You know, where it says you will tread on a snake."

His dad hugged him. "God sure keeps his promises, doesn't he? I stepped on that snake and it didn't harm me."

Once again we thanked God for guarding Dave's dad.

"We'd better skin this snake," said Jon's dad. "It'll be a reminder to us of this trip and God's promises from Psalm 91." He took his knife and skinned the snake in under five minutes, showing off the skills that made him such a good surgeon.

We threw the carcass to one side and salted the skin, and stretched it next to the first. Just then we heard a snuffling, dragging noise. Matt pointed the flashlight beam in the direction of the noise and we all saw a hyena loping away carrying the skinless snake in its mouth. My heart thumped wildly.

"God's garbage collectors," my dad laughed. I looked at him and wished I wasn't so afraid of things like hyenas and snakes. Then the thought struck me.

"Hey dad, we both killed a puff adder today," I said.

"You're right, Dean. God sure gave you courage this morning. I tell you, I was scared walking through the bush tonight, expecting the snake to jump out at me any second. But I prayed and God gave me the strength to go on."

I'd never thought of my dad as being scared before. Maybe it wasn't so bad to be scared, as long as I didn't let my fear control me.

"Let's get to bed, boys," Matt's dad ordered. "We have lots to do tomorrow."

This time when we crawled under the sleeping bag, we fell asleep right away.

CHAPTER SEVEN

Poachers

I woke the next morning with Matt's knee ground into my thigh. I groaned and pushed his knee away. "Ooooh!" he complained groggily. "I ache all over. Dean, you had your elbow in my stomach half the night."

"You weren't such a good pillow yourself," I countered, rubbing my thigh. "And my side aches from falling off the Land Rover." After pulling on cold socks and shoes, we stumbled outside into the sunlight. The warmth of the sun began to ease our aches and pains. Jon's dad looked at my side and said it was bruised and would be sore for a day or two but it would heal quickly. The best thing I could do was to walk and move normally to loosen up the muscles.

We ate our breakfast—dry cereal and

roast wart hog—and then discussed plans for the day. We all agreed that despite some discomfort, we had managed to sleep. We Rhinos wanted to stay on as planned. So the four men would drive back to the Ranger Post and report the robbery and buy some food to supplement our meat. We boys would stay around camp until they came back. In the afternoon we'd make another hunting trip, this time trying to find a Thomson's gazelle.

We Rhinos planned to track down the robbers and find out what had happened to Skeezix. I desperately wanted to tell my dad, but I didn't dare. He and the other dads might forbid us to go, and then the other Rhinos would blame me. So I bit my tongue and felt miserable. I was scared. Even worse, I knew I was deceiving my dad. We agreed to guard the camp and waved goodbye as they drove away.

As soon as they'd passed the first bend in the road, Matt said, "Let's get going, guys. Jon, start casting around for tracks. Dean, write a note telling our dads where we've gone. Dave and I will fill our canteens and roast a few slices of meat so we can carry them with us for lunch."

I wrote a brief note saying we'd gone

searching for Skeezix and attached it to the flap of our dads' tent, using a long thorn. By the time I was done, Jon called out that he'd found tracks. Dave and Matt stuffed the half-cooked meat into a plastic bag and we ran off.

"I had a tough time finding anything," Jon said. "Our dads tromped out any tracks near camp with their snake hunt last night. It looked almost like a herd of buffaloes had been trampling through here. But near the river I found distinct footprints of bare feet. But no dik-dik tracks anywhere. My guess is they carried Skeezix away."

"What are we waiting for?" Matt demanded. "Let's go."

Following Jon, we began tracing the trail left by the people who had raided our camp the day before. I prayed silently that God would be with us. I even found myself hoping Jon would lose the trail as he'd done when we'd once tracked smugglers on Kenya's coast. My side still hurt, but the walking had loosened up the muscles and the pain was now a dull ache.

After about an hour and a half, Jon suddenly motioned for us to stop. Then he ducked down. We all copied him, then crawled on our bellies until we lay side by side.

"What is it?" whispered Matt.

"I saw some smoke up ahead near that cliff," Jon said, pointing. We looked and saw the wisps of white smoke curling up into the cloudless sky.

"Is it a campfire?" I asked quietly.

"I think so," Jon answered. "But I don't know who it belongs to. It might be the people who robbed our camp. Or it could be some Maasai herdsmen cooking a goat for lunch."

"I think we should head back to camp and then bring our dads here to investigate," I suggested, feeling a knot in my stomach.

"We have to find out exactly whose camp this is first," said Matt. "Let's edge closer and see who's making that smoke. If it looks like it's the guys who robbed us, we'll sneak away and come back with our dads. Now come on, there's nothing to worry about."

"I'm with Dean," Dave whispered. I turned, surprised. "Not that I'm scared," Dave went on, "though I don't think Dean's all that scared either. I'm just being practical. Even if we get close, how can we tell if they're the ones who robbed us? I think we're taking too much of a risk. We know where this place is. Let's quietly head back to camp and bring our dads out here."

"Nothing doing," Matt said, even more

pig-headed than usual. *Maybe all that warthog meat is going to his head and not his stomach,* I thought to myself. "We're going to find out who's making that smoke. If it is the guys who messed up our camp, we'll probably see things like our sleeping bags laying around. Then we can give our dads a solid report, not some story about seeing smoke. I think you two are just scared. Dave, you and Dean can stay here. Jon and I will move closer to see what's going on."

Matt's words got to me. "I'm coming too," I said. Dave was at my side, nodding grimly. He wouldn't be left behind, either.

Hunching forward, we crawled on our stomachs toward the smoke. My green, military-style canteen that hung on my belt kept banging as we crept closer. Jon flashed an irritated look at me and put his forefinger to his lips telling me to be quiet. Sweat dripping into my eyes, I pulled my canteen further back on my belt so it wouldn't clunk around.

Jon had pushed his way under a thick bush. We joined him. From there we had a clear view of the campsite. We could see three men squatted around a fire roasting meat. In my heart, I hoped they weren't eating Skeezix. We saw a pile of at least twenty zebra skins under a tarp. A stack of gazelle horns filled another area. A gunny sack lay partly open. We could see it held a heap of rhino horns. Guns stood leaning against a tree. A jumbled stack of wire and rope snares stood near the guns.

"Poachers," I whispered to the others. "Let's get our dads and report this to the game rangers.

At last, Matt agreed. "We can't do anything except get help. Poachers can be dangerous. Even if they didn't steal our stuff, they need to be caught with the evidence." He paused as if thinking. "You know," he went on, "if we all go get help, these poachers may move on. Or their contact man may show up with a truck to carry away all the animal trophies. Then even if the rangers come, the poachers will get away. Dean, you and Dave head back to camp. Jon and I will stay here and keep an eye on them until you get back."

I started to protest, "But, Matt..." Just then one of the men by the fire stood up and looked in our direction. We froze. The man spoke to his companions and one walked away in the other direction. The two remaining men settled back onto their haunches by the fire.

"You two had better go now," Matt

ordered. Dave and I slipped away. When we were a safe distance away, we stood up and started to run back to camp.

Suddenly a gunshot ripped through the air and we heard shouts coming from where we had left Jon and Matt.

Dave and I looked at each other. "Oh, no!" Dave breathed.

I whispered a prayer and said, "We'd better run faster, Dave!"

We sprinted through the bushes heading for camp.

CHAPTER EIGHT

Running for Help

As Dave and I crashed wildly through bushes to get help, I wondered if Matt or Jon had been shot. That thought gave me strength to keep running when my body, especially my sore side, shouted at me to stop and rest. I don't know if Dave wondered the same thing, but he kept running too.

After half an hour, Dave slowed down and stopped. I pulled up beside him. "What do you think happened?" I asked between gasps.

He shook his head. "I don't know, I just hope..." He couldn't go on. I put an arm on his shoulder and we both cried. Not much, but we couldn't stop the tears from leaking out. Our friends might have been killed.

"I need a drink," I said after a minute of

silence. We both took long pulls on our canteens, the water refreshing our dry throats.

"I've been praying the whole way for God to keep Jon and Matt safe," Dave said.

"Me too," I answered.

Dave went on, "My mind keeps going back to Psalm 91. Surely, if God kept his promises when he kept my dad safe after stepping on a snake last night, he will also be with Matt and Jon now."

I nodded in agreement. "God will keep them safe."

A noise in the bushes behind us startled us. "They're following us," Dave blurted, turning to run.

I joined him, smashing blindly into a whistling thorn bush.

I turned, expecting to see one of the poachers with a gun or a spear. Instead I saw a beautiful orange-red impala buck. The sight of me frightened him as much as his noise had frightened us. He turned to flee but stumbled and fell. Then I saw his problem.

"Dave, come back," I called. "It's just an impala." I gently eased my way out of the thorn bush, finding a few gashes in my arms and legs, but no deep punctures.

Dave and I approached the impala that now lay thrashing wildly on the ground. His back legs were hopelessly wrapped up in a mass of rope and wire. From one of the wires hung a wooden stake, still wet from the dirt where it had been anchored. Every time the impala struggled, the wire dug deeper into a bleeding wound in his leg.

"He must have been caught in a poacher's trap," Dave said, examining the animal's leg. "Somehow he managed to pull the trap out of the ground, but now he's so tangled in the trap he'll die if we don't release him." He reached for the impala's legs to free him but the impala used his front legs to scramble away. Then he lay down, exhausted and frightened.

"You'll have to hold his front end, Dean," Dave said.

I looked at the impala's curving horns with sharp tips. "How can I hold onto him without getting poked by his horns?" I asked.

"Just do it, Dean. We can't leave him like this. And we have to get help for Matt and Jon," Dave pleaded.

I reached for the impala's head. He lunged out at me and his forehead and nose hit me right in the chest. Instinctively, I grabbed on. I was right between the spread of his horns. I closed my eyes and gripped tighter. If I let go, I could get hit by the point of one of his horns. He pulled right and left, but when I held him firmly, he submitted and lay trembling against my chest.

"Good job, Dean," Dave said quietly. He hacked away at the rope and wire that trapped the impala's legs. Within a few minutes the impala's legs were free.

"I've got it," Dave said. "You can let him go, now, Dean."

"How?" I asked.

Dave laughed.

"What's so funny?" I asked, still clinging to the impala's head with my chest between his horns.

"I wish I had a camera," Dave said, still laughing. "If you could only see what you look like."

By now the impala had realized its back legs were free and he struggled to his feet. As he did, I let go and leaped backward, landing on my rear in the dirt.

The impala gave us a puzzled look. Then he walked, carefully at first, but then with more confidence. I moved toward Dave. As I did, the impala bounded into the air and crashed through the bushes.

"Makes you feel good, doesn't it?" I commented to Dave.

He nodded his agreement. "Now, let's get back to camp and get help."

We ran again, though not as fast as at first. Half an hour later we met our dads just unloading the food they'd bought.

"Dad! Poachers!" I hollered when I saw him. "Matt and Jon may be caught; may be shot." Then I collapsed into his arms.

"Dean, what are you talking about?" he asked.

My chest heaved with both emotion and tiredness. So did Dave's. But after we took a few deep breaths, we managed to tell our dads what had happened. We could see by the concerned look on their faces that Matt and Jon were in serious trouble.

Matt's dad started organizing things right away. He told my dad and me to drive back to the ranger post and bring some game rangers in the Land Rover. Dave would lead him and the other men on foot to the poachers' camp where they'd try to rescue Matt and Jon if they were still alive.

I would guide the Land Rover with my dad and the rangers to the poachers' hideout, and they could arrest the poachers.

"Let's pray before we head out," my dad said, and he led us in one of his efficient prayers that he saved for emergency situations.

Taking three of the guns, the others began hiking toward the poachers' camp.

We waved as we headed the Land Rover back onto the dirt track to the ranger post.

After a tooth-rattling ride, we pulled up in a swirl of dust in front of the ranger post. My father swung out of the door and ran into the small office. I followed him in and listened to him explain in Swahili what had happened. A two-way radio crackled on a table in the office. A yellowing calendar hung on the wall above the radio. It was two years out of date and encouraged people to have smaller families.

After listening to my father, the ranger in charge shook his head. "Too dangerous," he said. "You say these poachers have guns. We have to report this to the police in Narok. When they come, we can go and arrest these poachers."

My dad was frustrated. "How soon will that be?" he asked.

The man shrugged. "Maybe tomorrow," he answered. "First I have to get a ride into Narok. Then I have to persuade them to come. Then, if they decide it's important, they'll come. Maybe tomorrow. Maybe the next day."

"But these poachers have two of our

children!" my dad pleaded. "Can't you call them on the radio and get them to come right now?"

"Oh, no," the ranger replied. "The radio is only for official business." He reached over and switched it off. "Now, just go back to your camp and wait. I will contact the police and we will take care of this small problem." He smiled and guided us toward the door.

Another ranger who had witnessed the whole thing looked embarrassed. Once outside, the head ranger said goodbye and entered his office and shut the door.

On our way out, Dad said, "Looks like we'll have to do it ourselves, Dean."

The ranger who had looked embarrassed said softly, "We'll help."

Dad looked at him sharply. "What?..."

"Just drive to that chai [tea] house over there. The one with the name Ole Dume on it. Order some chai and wait for me."

With that he disappeared behind the office to some wooden buildings at the back of the ranger post.

CHAPTER NINE

Kidnapped

We stopped in at the chai house and sat at a wooden table, damp from many wipings, and ordered chai. I loved Kenyan chai—warm, milky, and sweet. But I couldn't enjoy this cupful, thinking of the danger two of my best friends were in.

"What's going on with the rangers?" I asked my dad. "I mean, the head guy said they couldn't help, yet this other one told us to come here and wait."

"I'm not sure, Dean," my dad answered. "I just know the second ranger didn't want his boss to know he's meeting us." He looked at his watch. "If he doesn't come soon, we'll have to join the others and try to rescue Matt and Jon ourselves."

Just then the ranger stepped into the chai

house with two others carrying guns. He sat at our table. "My name is Menta Ole Dume. My brother owns this chai house. We are both Ole Dume, sons of Dume. After reading the magazines you left at the Post yesterday, we realized you are Christian missionaries. I, too, am a Christian. I am saved and Jesus is my Savior. These other two are also Christians," he said pointing at his companions. "We want to arrest these poachers and get your sons back."

"But the ranger in charge said you couldn't go without the police," my dad questioned.

"That man is the poachers' partner," said Menta, with a dark frown on his face. "He works for the government to protect and control animals. Yet he protects poachers if they will spit in his palm," Menta went on, referring to the common practice of bribery. "We know this is wrong, but it's hard to fight against it because he has many friends in high places. But now, with your children in the hands of the poachers, we must act."

We went from the dark gloom of the chai house into the brilliant sunshine and climbed into the Land Rover. I sat between the front bucket seats, and Menta sat beside me. He asked me to describe the place where we'd seen the poachers' hideout. I told him and he nodded.

"I know the place," he said. "We have often seen the remains of poachers' camps there, but we've never been able to catch them. I think my boss warns them when we are coming."

Menta looked at my dad. "I know a short-cut to this place," he said and began giving directions. There was no road, so my dad had to avoid stones, ant hills, trees, and ant bear holes. It slowed us down, but he threaded his way through the bush until Menta told him to stop. "No closer or they'll hear the car," he said.

We had come around the back side of the camp. In the distance we could see a sheer drop. "The camp will be below that cliff," Menta said.

I realized we were now above the camp, not below it where we had first approached.

Crouching, Menta and his two partners ran toward the cliff.

"Stay back," my dad warned me. "There may be shooting." He didn't have to tell me twice.

We could see Menta throw himself down behind a large boulder. He peered down over the cliff, his gun ready. Then he stood up and waved us to come on. "They have gone," he called. "There is no one here."

Just as he finished saying that, a shot rang out. Menta dropped to the ground.

"The poachers are up there," we heard a voice shouting. "I think I hit one."

My dad had thrown me to the ground under him at the sound of the shot. But on hearing the voice he jumped up. "That's Matt's dad," he said. "I recognize his voice." Then he shouted, "It's us. We're not poachers. Dean and I are here with the rangers. Hold your fire."

He then knelt down by Menta. "Are you hurt?" he asked.

Menta smiled. "No, I just jumped to avoid any more bullets. Your friend can't shoot very well, can he?"

"His son is one of the boys the poachers have taken. He's very worried," my dad answered. "I'm sorry he shot at you, but I'm thankful you weren't hurt."

We went to the edge of the cliff and saw Dave and the other three men. Dave's dad called up, "Is everyone okay up there?"

We said yes and clambered down the cliff.

When we were reunited, Matt's dad explained, "We had just arrived and were trying to sneak up on the camp. It looked empty, but we thought the poachers might have set up an ambush. Then we saw the ranger move on top of the cliff. I fired without thinking." He turned to Menta and apologized.

Menta smiled and said, "If my son were missing, I would have done the same." Looking around, he said, "It looks like the poachers ran away with your boys. This camp has been abandoned. They must have realized when someone knew the boys were missing they'd follow them here. Let's search the camp to see if we can find any clues to where the poachers have gone."

"They didn't leave with a vehicle," Jon's dad said. "We've circled the camp and found no wheel tracks."

"We only saw three men when we watched them cooking a meal," I said. "Even if they made Matt and Jon carry stuff, there's still no way they could have cleared out the camp so fast."

"That's right," agreed Dave. "Right here was a pile of zebra skins. We saw a sack of rhino horns over there. And remember the stack of gazelle horns and the jumble of snares?"

"And they had a tent and guns," I added. We all searched, but could find nothing.

Even the campfire was nothing but a heap of cold ashes.

"It's almost as if you dreamed the whole thing," Menta commented.

"But they were really here," I protested.

"I know," Menta said, soothing me. "I believe you. But these poachers are really clever. Tell me, did you notice whether they had a radio?"

"I didn't see one," Dave answered. I said I hadn't either.

"But we couldn't see inside their tent. They could have had a radio in there," I said.

"Well, we won't learn much more from this camp," Menta said. "And the poachers are such clever bush men they will have covered all signs of their leaving so we can't track them from here. We'll have to decide what to do next."

The men gathered together and started discussing their next move.

"I'm going to sit under that tree growing out of the cliff," I told Dave. "I'm hot."

Dave followed me. I sat down next to the tree and leaned against a rock. As I did, the rock slid away, and I felt myself tumbling backward into a deep, black hole!

CHAPTER TEN

Keeping Watch

I landed heavily on my back in thick dust. I heard Dave's voice calling after me. "Dean, are you all right?" His voice seemed to come from a distance.

"Yes, I'm fine," I yelled back after sitting up. I looked around. "I seem to have fallen into a cave of some kind." As my eyes adjusted to the gloom I could see what surrounded me.

"Dave," I hollered. "Get our dads! You'll never believe what I've found!"

Dave scrambled in next to me, and my dad's head appeared at the entrance to the shaft. "What's down there?" my dad asked.

"All the poachers' stuff," I answered.

"Yeah," Dave chimed in, "here's that stack of zebra hides and the gunny sack of rhino horns. Everything. Even our boxes of food and our sleeping bags."

"Everything except their guns," I added.

One of the game rangers climbed down with us and began hauling out the animal trophies. Dave and I helped until we had cleaned out everything except a tangle of wires used by the poachers for making snares. I took one last look around the cave and saw what looked like a small skin in the corner. I walked over to pick it up. I couldn't believe my eyes. "Dave!" I called. "Look, I've found Skeezix!" The baby dik-dik lay shivering, his eyes wet, soft and brown. I cuddled him and carried him out of the cave. We covered up the entrance to the hole so it looked like nothing had changed. Then we all climbed the cliff, carrying the poachers' loot to the Land Rover.

At the car, our dads had a council of war with the rangers. Matt's dad wanted to start tracking down the poachers so they could rescue Matt and Jon right away. Jon's dad supported him.

But Menta had another idea. "We can track them," he said. "But they have their guns and your sons. It would almost certainly end in a gunfight and someone could get hurt. Or they might use your boys as hostages. I think it would be best to set up a guard around this camp. They will return. They left their food here and all their animal trophies. I think they'll return soon. I've never seen such a pile of animal hides and horns. To me, that means their contact will be coming soon to transport everything away and smuggle it out of the country."

He stopped speaking. A look of deep sadness came over his face. Then he continued, "To shoot an animal to eat is one thing. To slaughter hundreds so some person overseas can have an animal trophy makes me sick. These poachers would be forced to stop if no one bought their trophies. It's true, the poachers do the killing. But the middlemen and the overseas buyers are guilty as well."

Dave's dad responded, "If we wait here until they return, we may be able to catch not only the poachers but also the merchants who smuggle the goods out. The animal death merchants."

"But Matt and Jon..." began Matt's dad.

Menta said, "I know you're worried about your children. I am a Christian just as you are. Believe me, the best we can do for them now is to pray for their safety. I am certain these poachers have a time arranged to meet the buyers. You remember I told you my boss at the ranger post wasn't willing to help you because I believe he's involved somehow with selling these animal trophies. I overheard him on the radio last night and he said, 'One more day and then we'll have to pick up everything. Is the money ready?' I suggest we all get in the Land Rover and drive away. Then we'll come back on foot and set up a guard ready to ambush the poachers when they return. And, with the Lord's help, we'll be able to rescue your sons as well."

Everyone agreed it was the best we could do for now. Before we climbed into the Land Rover, we prayed earnestly for Matt and Jon. Then we drove away, kicking up a swirling dust storm behind the four-wheel-drive vehicle.

We hid the car about a mile away and ate lunch and drank gallons of water. I wasn't very hungry, but the sweltering heat had given me a fierce thirst. After lunch, Menta divided us into groups and we followed different paths back to the poachers' hideout. Dave and I were in one group with all our dads. Menta had chosen our group for what he thought would be the least hazardous duty. We were instructed to sneak up to about a hundred yards away from the poachers' camp and hide underneath some yellow fever trees near the river. Menta didn't think the poachers could possibly return from that direction. Yet it gave us a good view of the camp and we could signal the others if we did see something. The game rangers covered the other approaches to the camp, with two of them behind the rocks on top of the cliff above the cave.

We separated and made our way to our appointed places. Finding the trees Menta had spoken of, we cleared out some of the bush and bunkered down to watch.

The afternoon sun was hot and I soon had sweat dripping down my forehead. A fly buzzed around my head before attempting to land on my nose. I smashed at it, injuring my nose instead. The fly droned off. Soon his brothers and cousins swarmed all around, making us miserable.

"Does anyone have bug spray?" I asked. No one did, so we endured the flies. As it grew later, the flies tired of us and left. Nothing had happened. We could not see any of the other groups. We did our best to sit quietly and wait.

I looked up in the sky and saw a sign that is as well known in Africa as are the golden arches in America. "Look at the vultures," I whispered, pointing at the black shapes circling an area a few miles off from where we were hidden. "Something's dead."

Of course, it could be anything from a lion's kill to an animal that died of old age. But in my mind, I saw the poachers. Maybe they'd shot something for lunch. Or maybe... I didn't want to think about it, but maybe. I had a picture in my mind of Jon or Matt's body being picked on by squabbling vultures.

A verse I'd memorized for Sunday school came into my mind. "Cast all your cares on him for he cares for you." I began praying for Matt and Jon.

"Dear God, don't let them die. Please, God," I pleaded.

The sun began to set. My dad passed around some meat he'd carried along and we chewed on it for a while. Then we passed around a canteen. The sky turned orange as the setting sun shot its dying rays through the dusty horizon. Then it was dark. In the distance a hyena whooped.

Still we waited. My dad took out the flashlight so he'd be ready to signal the others if we saw anything. But nothing happened.

My clothes, damp from my earlier sweating, clung clammily to my body as the cold

African night crept around us. I shivered. My dad put his arm around me and held me close. I began to feel warmer. What had started out as such a great hunting trip was ending in disaster. I couldn't understand why God let things like this happen. I looked up at the stars that lit the sky. I remembered the song we'd sung the night before about God's greatness seen in the stars. But where was he now? I shook my head.

Just then the bushes behind us rustled and a branch snapped.

CHAPTER ELEVEN

Planning an Ambush

I had a hard time swallowing my heart, which seemed to have crawled into my mouth for safety. Dave's dad turned quickly and pointed his gun at the area where we'd heard the noise. My dad aimed the flashlight but didn't turn it on. He told me later he hadn't wanted to give away our position in case it was only an animal.

We kept still and listened. We heard a soft thumping noise and a muffled snuffling. Then a voice saying in English, "I have to make it. I just have to make it."

I recognized the voice at once. "It's Jon!" I said in a harsh whisper. "Jon! Jon, we're over here."

Jon tumbled into his dad's arms and cried softly. "I can't believe I made it."

Jon's dad said in a trembling voice,

"Thank God you're safe. I've been praying and praying."

"I've been praying, too, Dad," Jon answered between sobs.

Matt's dad stood beside them. As the crying subsided, he asked the question we all ached to have answered. "Is Matt okay?"

Jon nodded. "He was when I escaped about an hour ago," Jon said. "I hope he's still fine."

"But what about the gunshot this afternoon when Dave and I left to get help?" I interrupted. "We thought the poachers had discovered you and shot at you."

Jon smiled faintly. "Well, neither of us were hurt by the gunshot, but it did lead to our being captured. One of the poachers had gone near the bush where we were hiding. We thought they'd seen us. Matt and I tried to blend into the ground. But there wasn't much we could do. When the gun went off, Matt jumped up and shouted, 'They're shooting at us! Run, Jon, run!'

"We both erupted out of the bush and ran directly into a poacher holding a .22 rifle. He was more surprised than we were! He'd gone hunting for guinea fowl in the bush behind us. He'd been shooting at the birds. He didn't even know we'd been hiding. I wish we'd stayed hidden."

"It's okay," his dad said putting his arm gently on Jon's shoulder. "What happened next? Did the poachers hurt you?"

Jon continued, "The man dropped his gun and grabbed us, calling for his friends to come help him. They took us back to their camp and tied us up while they discussed what to do. They asked if others were with us. We said no, but they laughed and said they knew children like us would not be out by ourselves. Besides, they said they'd been to our camp the night before and knew there were others. We told them our dads would come soon with game rangers to arrest them.

"Again they laughed. They said they knew the man in charge of the game rangers, so they had nothing to worry about. But they did seem a bit concerned. One kept saying he had children of his own and he knew our fathers would come looking for us. So they hid everything in a cave and then they herded Matt and me away to another camp hidden in the forest over there." Jon pointed, but in the darkness, we could see nothing.

"If they had you and Matt tied up, how did you escape?" I asked.

Jon explained proudly, "After we'd been in the forest for a while, they offered us some tea. We told them we needed to have our hands free to drink. They figured boys couldn't escape so they released us and we drank the tea while they watched us closely. But when they tied us up again I tried something I'd seen in a Mickey Mouse comic book. I took a deep breath as they looped the rope around my stomach and then held my hands tightly, like I was praying, when they tied my wrists. But I held the bottom part of my palms firmly apart. When they finished I released my breath and put my palms together. My trick worked! The ropes were loose!

"As it got dark, I kept wiggling my hands until they were free. Then I was able to slip the rope holding my waist to the tree down my body. Finally I reached down and untied my ankles. I had just begun helping Matt when one of the poachers left the campfire and walked toward us. Matt hissed at me to go find help, so I ran. The poacher shouted to the others that I had run away. They said not to try to catch me. The lions and hyenas would find me soon enough." He shivered at the thought. "I'm so glad I found all of you."

He reached around his dad and gave him a huge hug. Suddenly he pushed away from his dad. "I almost forgot! I have news to help us rescue Matt and catch the poachers."

Jon went on to explain how Matt had overheard the poachers talking about their plans to move the skins and horns that very night. A truck was coming from the south. It was scheduled to arrive at about two A.M. at the cave where they'd hidden the skins and other animal trophies.

On hearing this information, Matt's dad went and got Menta and they started planning. Menta said, "We were right about them coming back to the cave to get their things. But knowing where the truck is coming from will help. There's only one road coming in from the south. We can set an ambush for the truck just as it arrives on that track near the cave. Catching the men who do the smuggling will be more important than catching the poachers. If the poachers appear before the truck does, we can surround them in the cave and, hopefully, rescue your son. If the truck comes first, we'll get the smugglers. In the dark, we can't hope to catch all of them. I'm sure they'll scatter. Our biggest concern will be Matt's safety. Let's just pray they drop him while they run for their own lives. Let's pray now and then we'll hide ourselves again."

"And this time, we'll take a more active role," said Jon's dad. "We're moving closer to the cave with you and your rangers."

Matt's dad led in prayer, especially pleading with God to protect Matt. I kept remembering how God had protected us from stepping on snakes. I prayed in my own heart that God would protect all of us from the arrows (or bullets) that might fly.

Then the men went off to set the ambush for the truck. As we three Rhinos sat there alone, Dave handed Skeezix to Jon. "Look who we found in the cave," he said. Jon was delighted, and held the baby dik-dik and stroked its silky fur. Suddenly the dik-dik reached up and started sucking on Jon's earlobe.

"Poor thing. He's really hungry," Jon said, gently pulling the dik-dik off his ear. We sat silently as we thought of what might happen in the hours ahead.

"I wish there was something we could do," I said.

Dave didn't answer, but I could see him thinking. Suddenly he said, "There is something we can do. Jon, you stay here with Skeezix. Dean, come with me. We have to hurry to the poacher's cave and get some wire we left there. We need to set a trap of our own for the poachers when they run so we can rescue Matt."

I had no idea what Dave was talking about. But I knew if he had a plan for a trap, he would be able to build it. And when Dave built something, it worked. I hurried after Dave as we stumbled through the darkness toward the cave.

CHAPTER TWELVE

Setting the Trap

Neither of us talked as we hurried toward the cave where we'd left the poachers' snare wire. The half moon had just peeped over the horizon and helped us to see the path. We paused when we reached the entrance to the cave. Peering in, I said, "Dave, it looks kind of dark in there."

"You're right," he answered. "That's why I brought this." He pulled a small pen light from his pocket. "It was in my backpack that we got back from the poachers when we emptied the cave." The beam barely lit an area one foot in front of us. But we already had an idea of the layout of the cave and where the snare wire had been left.

We found the wire easily enough. As Dave knelt to start untangling it, he began telling me his plan. "Here, Dean," he said. "Hold this end of the wire while I get it loose from this stick. Now, I've been thinking that when our dads and the game rangers ambush the truck, the poachers will probably run for their lives. The punishment for poaching in this country is pretty stiff. Since they'll have Matt with them, I think at least one of them will grab Matt and take him, perhaps as a hostage, to protect himself. So I started to figure. Where would I run if I was a surprised and frightened poacher?"

"Where did you figure you'd run if you were a poacher?" I asked as we pulled another bit of wire loose. The piece I held had some animal fur stuck to it. I shuddered.

"The forest," Dave answered. "They'd have to run for the forest. It's the only place with enough shadows and cover for them to escape. With this moon, if they ran for the plains they'd be as easy to see as a pinching ant on white socks. They'd never make it. These days, the game rangers shoot to kill."

"I hope they won't," I said, "for Matt's sake."

"Well, anyway," Dave went on, "if they run for the forest, I've come up with a way to stop them. And save Matt, if we're quick." He began braiding two wire pieces at the ends to make a longer piece and told me to do the same.

He continued, "I figure if we put this wire at about a four-and-a-half to five-foot height and string it from tree to tree along the first row of trees in the forest, it should be about neck to chest high for most of the poachers. In the dark they'll never see the wire. If they're running fast, it will catch them and flip them on their backs."

I interrupted, "Just like the time I hit old Mrs. Cook's clothesline at a sprint when we were playing capture the flag at night."

Dave chuckled. "Actually, that's where I got the idea."

"Well, I know it can work. I can still feel the choking feeling I got after hitting that wire with my neck. The next thing I remember, I was flat on my back and you guys were pouring water on me and arguing about who would have to tell my parents I was dead," I said. Then I stopped. "But what about Matt?" I asked. "We don't want to hurt him."

"That's the beauty of this plan," Dave said. "Matt's short. If he's being dragged along by the poachers or forced to run, he'll go right under the wire. That's when we'll have to be quick and get to him while the poachers are down."

"You really have this thing figured out, Dave," I said admiringly. "Just like you always do."

Just then we heard a rock being kicked and voices talking in Swahili. Dave switched off his pen light and we backed against the wall of the cave and held our breath.

"I'm sure I saw a light," one of the voices said. "But it's gone now. We'd better have a look around."

My knees felt like butter in the sun. I slowly melted to the cave floor. The poachers had come earlier than we expected and Dave and I were trapped.

Dave knelt down beside me and held my hand tightly. I could feel he was trembling.

One of the men tripped. "It's dark in here," he said. "We should turn on our flash-light."

"No," his friend answered, "if we turn on our light we may alert the poachers and they'll abandon their plans for a pick up tonight."

Why are they talking about the poachers if they are the poachers, I wondered.

The first man said, "But if the light we saw was the poachers in here, they'll already know their cave has been raided so it won't matter anyway." And with that he switched his flashlight on. As he swung the beam around the cave it rested on the wall where Dave and I sat huddled in fear.

"It's the white boys," the man with the flashlight said, dropping the barrel of his rifle. "What are you two doing in here? Don't you know the poachers will be coming soon? You could have given away our whole trap."

Dave and I were so astonished to see two of the game rangers we could hardly speak. Dave stammered, "You, you, you see, we, we, we wanted to get some wire."

"You boys could be hurt," the other man said. "The poachers have guns and we have guns and it's night time. Your fathers told you to stay hidden and away from here. Now please go back. Now! And let's hope our lights have not disrupted our plans for catching the poachers and the men with the truck."

With that they escorted us out of the cave and back to where Jon had stayed with Skeezix.

"Boy, that was scary," I said shakily after the game rangers left. Dave told Jon how the men had seen our light in the cave and come to investigate and how scared we had been that they were the poachers.

"Too bad about your plan for a trap, Dave," I said.

"What do you mean, Dean?" Dave asked.

"Well, without the wire, how can we set the trap for the poachers who might run for the forest?"

Dave smiled and produced the wire from under his shirt. "I didn't want to try to explain to them so I just took what we needed. In the dim light, they never noticed. So now, both of you get busy and help me braid this wire together."

We worked hard to get the wire untangled, and when we had it ready we walked quietly to the edge of the forest and began stringing it from tree to tree. Dave tied it to a branch on the first tree. After that we wound it once around the next tree at the right height and went on. Soon we had a section almost fifty yards long wired and ready. We looked to where the cave was. This would be the quickest path from the cave to the forest.

We went back to our hideout behind a rock and prayed, asking God to help us rescue Matt. Then we sat back to wait. Dave and I kept thinking we heard the poachers but Jon would always say, "No, that's a bush baby," or "That's just an owl."

Shortly before one A.M., I heard a noise that sounded like a chain saw cutting wood. "Do you hear that noise?" I said excitedly. "It sounds like the truck is coming earlier than expected."

I looked at Jon and was surprised to see his eyes wide open in fear. I had never seen Jon afraid before.

"What's wrong?" I asked. "Are you afraid of the poachers and the men coming in the truck?"

"That's no truck, Dean," Jon said in a hoarse whisper. "That's the sound a leopard makes when it's prowling. And it's close!"

CHAPTER THIRTEEN

Ambush

"What do you mean, a leopard?" I asked, stepping closer to both Jon and Dave for protection. "Are you serious? It sounded like a truck with a loose exhaust pipe."

The sound cut through the night again, a rasping sound like a hand saw ripping through a board. This time I heard a soft grunt after each sound. This was no car.

I almost jumped into Dave's lap. The three of us huddled together with our backs to a tree. "What are we going to do?" I whispered.

Jon cut me off with a severe gesture to be quiet. I began to tremble. I tried to pray and remembered the verse from Psalm 91 which says, "You will tread upon the lion and the cobra." *Well, God helped us with the snake,* I thought. *I wonder about a leopard?* My mind filled with thoughts of being mauled and dragged up into a tree to be a leopard sandwich. *Surely, God, if you can save us from a lion, you can save us from a leopard. Please, God. We don't even want to step on him like it says in the verse. We just want him to leave us alone.*

I found I had squeezed my eyes shut. I opened them slowly and strained to see through the darkness. I looked at Jon and Dave. They sat silently.

We heard the sawing of the leopard again, this time much farther away. Whatever it wanted for supper that night, it wasn't three Rhinos or our baby dik-dik.

"I think it's okay to talk again," Jon said quietly.

"Thank you, Lord," I breathed. "You know, I prayed for God to save us from the leopard just like he promised in Psalm 91. I just changed the part about the lion to a leopard."

"I prayed the same thing," Dave said.

"Me, too," said Jon. "And God really answered. I know leopards rarely attack people, but when you're alone in the night and it's dark, well, a leopard coughing right next to you makes you a bit nervous."

"I wasn't nervous," I said. "I was plain scared!"

We all laughed a jittery, relieved kind of laughter.

We sat alert in the dark, waiting. But after about an hour we began to get sleepy. The next thing I remember was being pushed away by Dave who said in a sleepy voice, "Come on, Dean. Stop sleeping all over me."

I tried to sit up straight, but after a few minutes I nodded off again, this time on Jon's shoulder. He elbowed me off. "Dean, this isn't the time to snore in your sleep."

"But I never snore," I retorted. "If you want to hear someone snore, you should sleep with my little brother, Craig."

"Well, you sure snored just then," answered Jon. "And now you're doing it again."

"But I'm *awake,*" I protested. "How could I be snoring?" Then I heard it, too. "It sure sounds like someone's snoring," I agreed. "But it's not me. I'm talking!"

Jon listened carefully. "It must be the truck," he whispered. We all stood up, fully awake. We pushed our way to the edge of the bushes so we could have a view of the flat area in front of the cave. In the half moon, everything stood out clearly with a pale tinge over the whole scene. I strained to see our dads or the rangers. But even knowing where they were hiding, I could see nothing. The trap was well set.

The roar of the truck grew louder and we could see the harsh glare of headlights dancing up and down as the truck bashed its way up the rutted road.

Suddenly I spotted movement to our right. Four men carrying guns emerged from the trees and strode quickly toward the cave. They were followed by another man leading Matt who stumbled as he tried to keep up. Jon started to lunge forward, but Dave caught him.

"We have to help Matt," Jon whispered fiercely. "I know what it's like to be tied up and led like a donkey."

But Dave held Jon tightly. "We have to be patient. If we went out now, we'd ruin the surprise ambush and get ourselves caught just like Matt. I sure hope the poachers don't go into the cave before the truck comes or they'll know something's wrong when they see their stuff is missing. Then it will get really confusing if our dads and the rangers try to catch them just as the truck drives up."

To our relief, the poachers sat down with Matt by the entrance of the cave. One of them lit a cigarette. A few minutes later, the truck drove up the road where Jon had said it would come. It stopped and blinked its headlights three times. I thought I saw a flashlight blinking back from the cave but just then the rangers leaped out and surrounded the truck. Things happened so quickly after that, everything kind of got confused!

I could see two of the rangers jerking the door of the truck open. They reached in and yanked out the two men from the front seat. They grabbed the two men by the back of their jacket collars and quickly dragged them out of sight behind the truck.

The headlights from the truck continued to glare straight at the entrance to the cave where the poachers sat. From the direction of the lights, I guessed the poachers would have been blinded like an antelope in the road. They must not have seen the men in the truck being surprised and caught. I continued to stare at the cave. Then I did see a flashlight blinking from the cave. Apparently the poachers were waiting for a further signal from the truck. But the headlights stayed on with a steady beam.

The flashlight blinked again. A poacher stepped forward. We could hear him talking in Swahili to his friends. "They must have forgotten the signal. Or maybe they're drunk again."

He started walking carefully toward the truck. As he reached it, he opened the door and looked in. Turning back to the others, he shouted, "Something's wrong! They're not in the truck!"

The poacher smoking the cigarette stood up. "Look around the back, man. They must be there somewhere. The truck couldn't have driven itself."

As the first man stepped behind the truck I heard a muffled thump. Then a feeble, "Run, man, run!"

The second man dropped his cigarette and fired a shot toward the truck which ricocheted crazily off the metal. Then he turned and hurtled toward the forest. Within seconds, the other three men shot out of the cave, one of the men carrying Matt on his back like a back pack. One shot cracked from above the cave, but then I heard Matt's dad shouting, "No, don't try to shoot. They're using Matt as a shield."

The poachers raced toward the forest, just as Dave had predicted. We watched, waiting to hear the sound as the poachers crashed blindly into our wire trap.

As the first poacher approached the line of trees I noticed Dave licking his lips. But suddenly he was into the trees and out of sight. He was quickly followed by the next man.

"Something's wrong!" I blurted out. "The trap didn't work."

CHAPTER FOURTEEN

Rescue

"They're running just to the right of where we started stringing the wire," Dave said grimly. "I know one way to make the trap work."

And with that Dave ran out of the bushes shouting wildly and throwing stones. The next poacher shot his gun in Dave's direction, but since he was running, his shot went high. Dave threw himself on the ground. I looked up at the poachers. Sure enough, they had veered to the left. A few seconds later I heard a grunt. The third poacher had hit the wire. He landed flat on his back and his gun flew into the bushes. The last man, who carried Matt on his back, had no chance to see what had happened. He, too, ran headlong into the wire which caught him right across the neck. It snapped him onto his back and he fell heavily on top of Matt.

Jon grabbed me and said. "Let's get Matt before the poachers have a chance to recover." As we ran through the bushes, Dave jumped to his feet and joined us.

We arrived on the scene where both poachers rolled on the ground trying to get air. Matt lay still on the ground, moaning. I grabbed his legs while Dave and Jon took his shoulders, and we carried him away into the bushes. Then Jon started yelling for our dads and the rangers to come since we'd caught two of the poachers.

We saw flashlights bobbing and heard shouts as the rangers ran across from near the cave.

"Down by the forest," Jon shouted again.

I looked back and saw one of the poachers struggle to his feet and start a swaying run into the trees to our right.

"He's getting away," I cried out.

Menta had seen him and sprinted after him.

"Watch out for the wire!" Dave shouted. "Go to the right! The right!"

Menta obeyed instinctively and with a burst of speed caught up with the poacher and speared him with a headlong rugby tackle. The two men sprawled to the ground and out of sight in the darkness of the forest. But within a few seconds Menta emerged, pushing the poacher, who wore ragged shorts and a dirty brown t-shirt, in front of him.

The other rangers picked up the other poacher and carried him toward the truck.

"What happened to these two poachers?" Menta asked as he passed by where we were huddled over Matt. "And is your friend okay?"

Dave told Menta about the wire trap and how the poacher carrying Matt had hit it and fallen backward on top of Matt, who was still out cold.

By now our dads had arrived. Matt's dad bent over and cradled Matt's head in his arms. Then Jon's dad checked for Matt's pulse.

Jon's dad flicked open Matt's eyelid and shone his flashlight into his eye. At this, Matt groaned again and shuddered.

Then he sat up suddenly. "Oh, man, do I have a headache!" he said. "What happened?"

All of us began explaining at once, Dave telling about the trap, Jon talking about how Dave had thrown rocks and yelled at the poachers so they ran into the wire. I told how the poachers had been flipped into the air.

Matt sighed. "I didn't understand a word you all said. But if all the Rhinos are here and our dads are here, I guess I'm safe and everything's all right."

We all smiled and nodded. Jon's dad said Matt hadn't suffered any serious damage from being squished under the poacher. Matt's dad picked him up and we walked toward the truck.

We heard Menta clucking his tongue behind us. "That's quite a trap you boys set up," he said, plucking on the wire as if it were a guitar string. "It's no wonder it stopped those two men. They're lucky they didn't break their necks. How did the other two escape?"

"They ran to the right of where we started stringing the wire," Dave said. "I thought I'd calculated where they'd run, but they surprised me and bolted right past the wire."

Dave's dad put his arm on Dave's shoulder. "You did well, Dave. You stopped two of them and rescued Matt as well."

When we got to the truck, the men took stock of the situation. Menta said, "We have the two men from the truck who seem to be the leaders of this poaching ring. Then we have one poacher who came to the truck to see what was happening. And two more with very sore necks, caught in the boys' trap. I don't think we have much chance of finding the other two tonight, even with the moonlight.

"Let's tie this group up and put them in the truck. Then we'll drive back to your camp, picking up your Land Rover on the way. I don't trust our commanding officer. We're pretty sure he's the one who gave this group their signals by radio. So we'll take these men to Narok tonight with all the evidence that's in your Land Rover."

We all jumped into the truck and Menta drove slowly back to our camp. On the way he stopped by our Land Rover and my dad got out and drove it ahead of the truck. At camp we helped the rangers pile the skins, horns and other trophies into the back of the truck. Two of the rangers, guns in hand, sat next to the five poachers, who were tied up like the impala Dave and I had saved from the snare.

We sorted out our sleeping bags and other gear the poachers had stolen. Then Menta and his men were ready to leave. "We can't forget to thank God for his protection tonight," Menta said.

Our dads gathered us into a circle and we

each prayed a short prayer of thanks to God. I thanked God for saving us from the arrows and bullets that fly by night. Menta closed with special praise to God for his power.

Then the rangers drove off, following another road which would not lead by the ranger post. They didn't want to tip off the head ranger.

We dragged our sleeping bags to our tents. I yawned. "What a day," I said. "I'm tired. But I don't feel like I can sleep. What time is it, anyway?"

Dave, who always had on his special digital watch that could tell you what time it was any place in the world, said it was four A.M.

"I'm hungry," said Matt. "The poachers didn't feed us very much."

His dad laughed. "You're always hungry, Matt. Hey, we still have warthog meat. Why don't we build up our fire and roast some right now?"

My dad said he'd brew some cocoa to help us fall asleep after we ate, because we were all pretty keyed up.

As Jon's dad began slicing chunks of meat, we heard the sawing sound again. Jon said, "Get your gun, Dad. There's a leopard out there. And I think it likes the smell of our dinner."

CHAPTER FIFTEEN

Rescuing Animals

Our dads quickly herded us into the Land Rover and shouldered their guns. My dad turned on the Land Rover, revved the engine, and flicked on the headlights, hoping this would scare away the leopard.

Jon, with his quick eyes, spotted the leopard first. He opened the window and hissed to his dad, "Over by that tree, Dad. I can see the leopard's eyes glowing green in the light."

We all looked where Jon had pointed. The green eyes looked like a horrible version of the Cheshire cat from *Alice in Wonderland*. But soon, out of the shadows, the leopard's body appeared.

"He's limping badly," Jon stated. "Something's wrong with his front right paw."

"And he's skinny," said Matt, "like he hasn't eaten for days."

As the leopard hobbled closer, we could see he had no front right paw. There was only a jagged flap of skin where his powerful, needle-sharp clawed foot should have been.

Our dads tried to scare the leopard away, but he kept coming. Closer and closer. Dave's dad put his rifle to his shoulder and took aim. The leopard stopped as if to say, "Go ahead. I've had enough pain. Get it over with."

Slowly, Dave's dad lowered his gun. The leopard walked right past the men to the table near the fire where we'd been cutting meat. He reached up and tore into the meat. Then he lay down and licked the stump of his leg where the paw should have been. Then the leopard slowly stretched out and went to sleep.

Our dads opened the car doors and got in. "Well, boys," my dad said, "I think we'll all spend the night in here."

"What do you think happened to the leopard's paw?" I asked.

Jon answered, "I think the leopard got caught in one of the poacher's snares. The only way he could get free was to gnaw off his own foot."

Dave's dad agreed. "I think you're right, Jon. You can see the ragged skin flap. Poor thing. He will never survive in the wild. He looks nearly starved to death. I probably should have shot him, but the look in his eyes was so sad I couldn't. And now he's sleeping. Who could shoot a sleeping leopard? No, let's just get some sleep and we'll decide what to do in the morning."

"Yeah," my dad replied. "Maybe by then the rangers will have returned and they can help us find a solution. If we leave the leopard wandering around hurt he may become a goat killer or even a man-eater."

None of us slept well sitting huddled in the Land Rover. When the sun came up, the leopard still lay sprawled out near our fire.

"I wonder if he's still alive?" I said. Matt got the idea of tossing a rock near the leopard. He did and hit the leopard on the back. The leopard sat up and gave a nasty snarl before stretching out again.

"I'm getting hungry," Matt said. "What are we going to do now?"

Just then the rangers drove up in their green Wildlife Service four-wheel-drive truck. They stopped and began to get out but we wildly pointed at the leopard, which sat up and twitched its tail, but had no strength to move.

Menta drove their truck beside ours and we explained the situation. He nodded. "We have a box trap at the station. We can go fetch that. Then we can shove the leopard into the trap and feed him until he regains strength."

"But what can you do with him?" Jon asked. "You can't release him. Without a paw, he will die or turn on humans."

Menta smiled. "I agree. But we wouldn't release him. In Nairobi there is an Animal Orphanage next to the Nairobi National Game Park. It's somewhat like an American zoo. But they specialize in nursing wounded animals back to health. If they can be released into the wild again, they are. If not, they give the animals a large, fenced area where they can live comfortably."

"Hey," my dad said, "how'd you get to drive your own Wildlife Service vehicle? Isn't your boss the only one who can drive it?"

Menta laughed, "I *am* the boss. At least for now. When we took the poachers and the smugglers to the police last night, they told the police my boss was the real kingpin of their organization. So the police came with us to our post and arrested him this morning. And as the most senior ranger left, I am in charge. At least until Nairobi headquarters appoints someone else. Now let me go get that trap."

We waited and sweated in the Land Rover, which was becoming a steam box in the hot sun. But we knew it was for a good purpose. We were all excited the leopard would be saved. The leopard rolled over on his back and looked at us.

When Menta came with the box trap, he and his men jumped out. They had put a chunk of raw meat in the trap. The leopard smelled it and within seconds he had entered the trap. Menta dropped the door and his men hoisted the trap into the truck.

We all jumped out of the Land Rover. "What's to eat, Dad?" Matt said again. It was funny how someone as short as Matt could always be so hungry.

"Are you all hungry?" Menta asked from behind the steering wheel of his truck. We all nodded.

"Then follow me," he said.

He drove off and we piled into our Land Rover to follow in the dust. "Where's he taking us?" Jon asked.

Our dads just shrugged. Jon's dad said, "All I know is it has something to do with food."

After half an hour we pulled up next to a Maasai boma, a thorn fence enclosure around a group of roundish red-mud houses.

Menta got out of the truck. "Welcome to my home," he said. He called for his wife, who came out of the small house and greeted us. He whispered some instructions to her and she rushed off.

Menta then ushered us into his home. We stooped over to enter and then found ourselves in a dark, smoky room. Some of us sat on the edge of low, cowskin beds, others on short wooden stools. A fire glowed in the center of the room inside three stones. The room had no chimney and only one window about four inches square. Menta's wife soon returned and boiled some milk for tea. When it was ready, she served it to us in yellow enamel mugs with red roses painted on the sides. Then another woman entered with some steaming ugali, a thick cornmeal porridge. A third woman came in with a stew made of small, chopped pieces of goat meat and potatoes. Menta said his brother had just slaughtered the goat in our honor.

Tears streamed down our faces from the sharp smoke produced by the leleshwa branches in the fire. But the tea was sweet and good. They served us large dollops of ugali in metal bowls and then poured the stew around the edges. We Rhinos were in heaven, wadding pieces of ugali into balls and then making dip holes with our thumbs and using the ugali balls to pick up the rich stew.

Ugali is a heavy meal, and soon all of us were full. We thanked Menta and then stumbled out into the fresh air.

Menta laughed. "What's wrong, boys, too smoky for you?"

"A bit," I answered.

"Come, I want to show you something," Menta said.

We followed him outside of the boma. Menta called some of his brothers and they brought their spears and rungus, wooden clubs with a round knob on the end.

"Let me show you how I used to hunt birds when I was preparing to become a warrior," Menta said. Pointing at a distant target, he danced forward a few steps and flung the rungu. It whistled as it turned end over end. Then it smashed into the target. He retrieved the club.

"Now you try it," he said. We all tried throwing the club but all of us failed to hit the target. Menta then instructed us in how to throw a Maasai spear. We tried. Jon did the best, which didn't surprise me.

By now our dads had joined us and they all tried spear throwing and club hurling as well.

Finally it was time to leave. Menta shook our hands and thanked us for our part in capturing the poachers. "We have one more big job tomorrow. Maybe you can help us," Menta said.

"What is it?" Matt asked.

"We are going to bring out one of the poachers and have him show us where all their wire snares are hidden. Usually they have lines of them surrounding good water holes. We could find some on our own, but not all of them. Anyway, we'll be driving all over the place and uprooting the snares. We'll be releasing any animals we find or catching hurt ones to take to the orphanage together with the leopard."

Matt looked at us. "What do you think, Rhinos?" We all nodded vigorously. "Then it's unanimous. We'll help you pull up snares tomorrow."

Then he stopped and looked at his dad. "Uh, if that's okay with you, Dad. I mean, can we? Please?"

His dad smiled. "Sure. In fact we'll all come along and help."

As we got into the Land Rover, we saw

Skeezix in the corner where we'd shoved him the night before. He looked sick. I picked him up. "Guys," I said, "I think Skeezix is dying."

Menta came up and asked me to give him the baby dik-dik. "He is hungry," Menta said. "But I have a mother goat that can nurse him back to health. I'll bring your pet to your camp tomorrow when we come to pick you up for the snare hunt.

On the way back to camp, I thought about Skeezix. "You know, guys," I said, "I think we should let Menta take Skeezix to the animal orphanage along with the leopard. I know we think he'd make a great pet. But he's so young. I don't think he'd make it without special help."

The others thought about it and agreed. "Yeah, it would be best," Matt decided. "Besides, we could always see Skeezix again. We could ask our parents to take us to the animal orphanage on our next trip to Nairobi, so we could check on our dik-dik and our leopard."

Back at camp, we went into our tents and crashed. It had been a very long time since we'd slept. "I can't wait until tomorrow," Jon said before falling asleep. "You know, it's even more fun *saving* animals than it is hunting them." We all agreed.

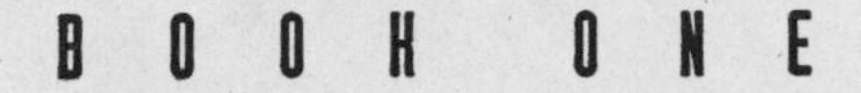

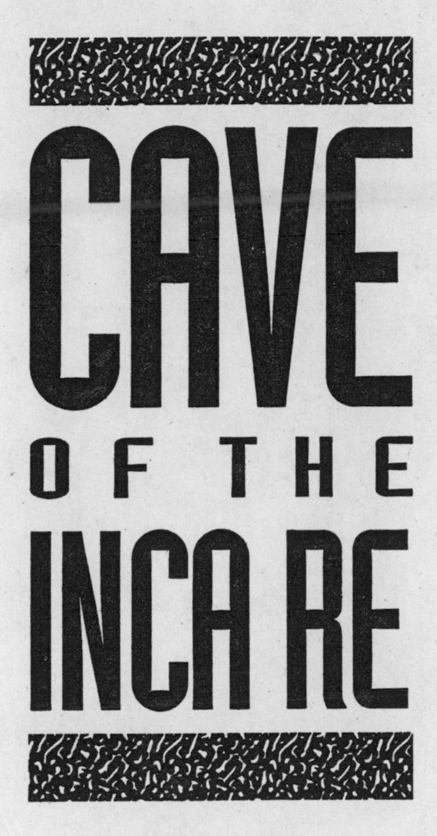

Editor's Note: The following is an excerpt from another Multnomah Youth three-in-one book, The Parker Twins: *Adventures in South America,* by Jeanette Windle. You can find this exciting book at your Christian bookstore!

PROLOGUE

A Desperate Decision

Glistening white in the silver light of a full moon, the massive stone walls of the ancient Indian city loomed ahead of the running children. Shouts of anger behind them told the pair that their escape had been discovered. Feeling like their lungs would burst, the two panting children ran along the outer wall of the main temple complex.

Pulling his sister to a halt at the foot of a narrow stone staircase, Justin peered around the crumbling blocks of stone carved by Inca craftsmen centuries ago. He jumped back as he caught sight of two shadowy figures running along the high wire fence that encircled the complex.

The clang of a metal-tipped boot echoed across the rough ground as one of the figures, a bulky outline against the shimmering dust of the stars, stumbled and fell against a dark boulder.

Cursing, he jumped to his feet. A moment later, a bright finger of light from an electric lantern probed the darkness behind the children.

"Come on, Jenny!" Justin hissed. He pushed his sister up the narrow steps that opened onto a vast courtyard. Dodging among the giant stone figures—tokens of long-past conquered nations—that dotted the open courtyard, the two children made their way toward the main entrance.

Suddenly both children startled with fear as a strangely high, thin voice echoed, seemingly inches away. Then they relaxed as they remembered the stone "loudspeaker" across the court where Inca priests had addressed the crowds that once filled this temple. Hidden behind a featureless granite figure, the children looked up anxiously at the wide-open grass strip that lay between them and safety.

A wispy cloud skittered across the face of the pale-gold ball above them. Taking advantage of the sudden shadow, Justin grabbed his sister's hand and yanked her across the open ground, and then through a wide, crumbled opening that had once been a door.

It was not a *real* door; it was just two weathered granite blocks on either side of a wide opening. A third stone block balanced on top of the other two to form a square entryway. Here, feather-caped warriors glistening with gold ornaments had guarded the temple hundreds of years ago.

A sudden cold beam of light told them their pursuers were again close behind. Holding hands, the two children sprinted for open fields beyond the courtyard, but Jenny stumbled and fell, her sudden cry alerting the men behind them. They froze for a moment, hoping no one had heard Jenny's cry. But seconds later they heard running feet.

Justin pulled Jenny to her feet. Reluctantly turning away from the open fields, the two children jumped over a shallow ditch the short rainy season had dug in the sandy soil. A solitary, evenly shaped hill lay before them. When they reached the base of the mound, no one was in sight. "I think we can slow down now," Justin wheezed.

But just as he spoke, a large, bulky figure rose from behind a jumbled pile of stone blocks only yards away. The white-gold rays of the full moon showed a cruel face smiling triumphantly.

"We've got you now," their massive pursuer gloated hoarsely. Justin glanced back toward the ruins. A short, skinny man walked unhurriedly toward the pair cowering against the hillside.

Justin tapped his sister on the shoulder. "Come on!" he whispered. Taking their would-be captors by surprise, the two children turned and quickly climbed the steep side of the mound. The two men went after them with hoarse, angry shouts, but the children had the head start they needed.

Above them, a large opening in the face of the hill had been sealed shut with cement bricks. Heavy boulders had been piled against the bricks as added insurance against intruders, but at one side a dark, ragged-looking area above the heaped-up boulders showed where a few bricks had crumbled away. Justin scrambled toward that spot.

Realizing where he was going, Jenny hesitated. "We can't go in there! We'll be killed!"

Justin was already squeezing through the small opening. "Yes, we can. God will protect us. Besides, there's nowhere else to go!"

He pulled his sister through the narrow hole, and the two of them backed into the darkness as a long arm reached in and groped for them. The men swore loudly. The opening was too small for either of them. They kicked against the bricks, but the solid wall resisted their kicking and pounding.

Jenny and Justin leaned against the stone wall of the cave, their chests on fire from the violent exercise. They hugged their thin jackets close to ward off the intense cold, and Justin remembered that this plateau sat at thirteen thousand feet—well over two miles above sea level. When they had climbed down from the airplane only a few days ago, they had gasped for breath after simply walking across the airport.

It was now quiet outside. The cave was pitch black, except for the faint moon-glow that shone through the opening. Anything could be hiding in that blackness, they knew. His arm around Jenny, Justin shut his eyes and tried to think.

How in the world did we get into this mess? he wondered desperately.

CHAPTER ONE

An Unexpected Visitor

sudden bang echoed through the one-story, cream-colored house as the kitchen door slammed hard. Mrs. Parker glanced up from the head of lettuce she was washing, frowning at the noise. "Justin Parker!"

The tall, husky thirteen-year-old flushed to the roots of his short-cropped red hair, and turned to shut the door again—more quietly this time. He knew his mother's strict rule against slamming doors. He paused a moment to breathe in the sweet, spicy fragrance coming from the oven, then threw a well-worn bat and baseball glove into the corner by the door. Tossing an equally well-used baseball up and down in one hand, he joined his mother at the sink.

"Mom!" he growled, his eyes stormy with annoyance, "you've got to keep Jenny out of my hair!"

Mrs. Parker moved to a wide work island in the center of the kitchen. Before she could answer, the door slammed again. A slim girl rushed into the kitchen. She too carried a baseball glove. Tossing it after her brother's, she leaned on the counter and pushed back heavy, dark curls that were slightly damp from running. Her golden eyes flashed fire.

"Mom, you've got to stop Justin from being so mean to me!"

Reaching for a small knife, Mrs. Parker, an older version of Jenny, calmly began slicing a tomato into a large wooden salad bowl. She didn't seem at all surprised at the storm.

"Why, I thought you two were the best of friends today. What happened?"

Before Jenny could open her mouth, Justin complained, "It's Jenny, Mom! You've got to keep her away when I'm playing ball with the boys. It's embarrassing! None of the other guys' sisters tag along!"

Jenny lifted an unapologetic chin and said huffily, "You know I can play better than any of them!"

There was truth in her words. Only a few minutes younger than Justin, his twin sister, Jenny, was as tall as he and a forward on her seventh-grade basketball team. She loved sports as much as she did books. Though in looks so much like her easygoing mother, Jenny seemed to move through life at a gallop.

At the moment, her height ran to long, slim arms and legs, but Jenny didn't have the awkwardness of many lanky girls. As she had said, she could beat most of the boys in the neighborhood in a foot-race or a baseball game.

Justin provided a good balance to the up-and-down moods of his sister. Calm and even-tempered most of the time, a stubborn streak kept him from being pushed around. His steady, hazel eyes noticed everything that went on around him, and he liked to think things through before talking.

Jenny, on the other hand, let everyone know exactly what she was thinking. "Justin used to like playing ball with me," she continued, now in a sadder tone.

"That was different!" Justin replied with exasperation. "The guys don't like girls hanging around during a ball game! I get teased about having Jenny along. You understand, don't you, Mom?"

Mrs. Parker sighed and laid her chopping knife beside the wooden salad bowl. Putting an arm around her angry daughter's shoulders, she said, "Jenny, there are times when boys like to play on their own without girls. You wouldn't like Justin tagging along all the time when you're playing with your girl friends, would you?"

"But that's the problem, Mom!" Sudden tears brimmed in Jenny's golden-brown eyes. "I don't *have* any girl friends now that school is out. There aren't any girls my age in the neighborhood—just boys! The only time I see my friends is in Sunday school. I get so bored playing by myself all the time while Justin is out having fun with the boys. It's not fair! Why should they mind me playing?"

Mrs. Parker cracked the door of the oven and inspected its contents, then lifted two pies onto the counter.

"Jenny, I'm sorry you don't have any friends close by, but you need to be more understanding of your brother. Let him spend some time alone with his friends. As for you, Justin, try to be more patient with your sister. It's hard for her this summer."

Her stern eye caught theirs, and they reluctantly nodded their heads. Glancing at his sister, a grin hovered on the corner of Justin's mouth. Being twins, Justin and Jenny had always been the best of friends.

"I have to admit, she really is the best catcher in the neighborhood, Mom." The grin spread across his freckled face. "You should have seen her! She grabbed a pop fly ball and got Danny Olson out just as he slid into home plate. I guess that's why the guys were so mad. If she'd miss occasionally, they'd think she was okay."

An answering smile banished the tears from

Jenny's eyes. "I'm sorry I teased you so much," she told her brother sincerely.

"Yeah, well, I'm sorry I yelled," Justin growled back. Apologies embarrassed him. "I don't mind you playing with us, but...the guys don't see it that way. Hey, the game's probably over by now anyway. Want to play catch until supper?"

Harmony restored, Justin gave his mother a hard hug, then collected his baseball equipment. Jenny added a quick kiss, then picked up her glove from the corner. Leaning over her mother's shoulder, she sniffed and inspected the two pies, oozing dark-red through slits in the top crust.

"Ummm, cherry pie! What's the special occasion, Mom?"

"Oh, didn't I mention it?" her mother answered. "We're having company for supper."

"Company? Who is it, Mom?"

Mrs. Parker swatted Justin's fingers with a pot holder as he reached for a dangling edge of golden crust. "I thought I'd keep that a secret for now," she said with a straight face.

"Aw, Mom!" the twins groaned in unison. "Come on, tell us!" Jenny added.

Their mother gave an exaggerated sigh. She knew she would have no peace until she told them, but she enjoyed teasing her two lively children once in a while. "Okay, I'll give you one hint. Your father just left for SeaTac airport."

"Uncle Pete!" the two chorused.

Seeing the smile that crept into her mother's eyes in spite of her attempts to look innocent, Jenny threw her arms around her mom. "We're right, aren't we?" she asked. Mrs. Parker nodded. "Yippee!"

Pete Parker, their father's brother, was Justin and Jenny's favorite uncle. A widower with no children, he was an executive of a large oil company, Triton Oil. He spent much of his time jetting around the world, troubleshooting for the company in different countries. Whenever he had free time, often at an hour's notice, he would fly into Seattle where his brother Ron worked as a computer analyst for Boeing.

The children were used to Uncle Pete's sudden appearances, and had a large collection of "treasures" he had brought them from all corners of the world. Like the twins' parents, Uncle Pete was a dedicated Christian. His special interest was missions, and he often visited missionaries in different countries while he was there on business. Jenny and Justin loved the stories he told of the strange and wonderful things that happened when these missionaries told people about Jesus.

Mrs. Parker smiled at her children's exuberance. "Okay, kids, you got what you wanted. Now get on out of here and give me some peace and quiet! Jenny, I need to have you back here in half an hour to set the table. Justin, it's your turn to do dishes.

"And put away your junk when you're done with it," she called out the screen door to their rapidly retreating backs. "I don't want to find it all over the yard!"

Justin had just scrambled over the fence to recover a missed ball when he heard the distinct rumble of his father's station wagon.

"Come on, Jenny. They're here!" he shouted, vaulting back over the fence. He tossed the ball and glove onto the front steps, but remembering his mother's plea, he picked them up again. Together they quickly stored the baseball equipment in its proper place in the garage.

By the time they had finished, their father had already pulled their dark-green station wagon into the garage and was stepping out of the driver's seat. Jenny threw herself into her tall, lanky father's arms. Upon meeting Mr. Parker, it was obvious to people how Justin came to have red hair and hazel eyes!

Ron Parker enthusiastically lifted his daughter from the floor and whirled her around. If Justin had inherited his coloring, it was Jenny who shared his outgoing personality.

"Hey, don't I get a hug, too?" Like his brother, Uncle Pete was tall and red-headed, but he was much broader. A full red beard made him look like a youthful Santa Claus. Slapping his well-rounded front, he liked to blame his size on the hospitality he couldn't refuse in the many countries he visited.

After greeting his nephew and niece, Uncle Pete reached into the back seat and pulled out the one small suitcase that was all he ever carried. "Something smells mighty good in your mother's kitchen," he declared. "Let's go eat, kids. I'm starved!"

▼▼▼

Gathered around the dining table, the family shared all that had happened since Uncle Pete's last visit three months earlier. Uncle Pete held out his plate for a second piece of cherry pie and leaned back in his chair.

"Helen, I haven't eaten so well since the last time I was here," he boomed.

The twins had been reasonably quiet during supper while the adults visited. Now they moved restlessly in their chairs. Jenny, who never hesitated to ask questions, burst out, "Do you have any new stories, Uncle Pete?"

"Yeah, where did you go this trip?" Justin added eagerly.

Uncle Pete's eyes twinkled at the impatient pair as he settled more comfortably into his chair. "As a matter of fact, I haven't been anywhere special since my last visit."

His red beard split in a smile at their disappointed look. "But I do have one little story that might interest you. What can you two tell me about the Incas?"

"Weren't they an ancient empire in South America?" Justin responded thoughtfully.

"Yeah, they built lots of stone cities. There was a picture in our history book last year of that secret stone city up in the mountains," Jenny added.

"Very good! You're both right. The city you're talking about, Jenny, is Machu-Pichu in Peru. In fact, a thousand years ago the Inca had one of the most advanced civilizations in the world. They governed from a high plateau in the Andes mountains around Lake Titicaca, the highest navigable lake in the world. Their empire spread over most of Bolivia, Ecuador, and Peru."

Uncle Pete stopped for a bite of cherry pie. Waving his fork, he continued: "The Inca were most famous for their stone cities and roads—all carved out by hand. Even today's technology can't beat their stone work, and a lot of their roads are still being used.

"But the Inca wasn't the first empire in South America. They took over from another great civilization—one that lasted three thousand years. Tiawanaku, the ruins of that civilization, still lies across Lake Titicaca, in the country of Bolivia."

He looked keenly at his nephew and niece. "Can you tell me what finally happened to the Inca?"

"Didn't Pizarro and just a couple of hundred Spanish soldiers defeat them?" asked Justin. "As I remember, they tricked them and captured their king, and the whole nation just gave up. It seems pretty cowardly to give in to two hundred men!"

"Well, that's what your history books may tell you, but it isn't the whole story. The Inca had a very advanced civilization but also a very cruel one. They conquered hundreds of smaller tribes around them and practiced human sacrifice with their enemies. Everyone but the Inca overlords were turned into slaves.

"When the Spanish arrived, these slave tribes rose up to fight beside them, hoping to win freedom from the Inca. So Pizarro didn't only have two hundred soldiers, he also had thousands of Indian rebels fighting with him. And he had cannon and gun powder, something the Inca had never seen."

"So what happened to the Inca after that?" Justin inquired.

"Their descendants are still there and so are the ruins of their empire. Imagine yourselves, kids, in the capital of Bolivia—the cold winds whistling through the stone walls of Tiawanaku...reed boats dancing across the waves of Lake Titicaca to ruined palaces of ancient Inca princes..."

Mrs. Parker, glancing in amusement at her

spellbound children, interrupted, "I take it you are visiting Bolivia soon?"

"You guessed it! Triton Oil has several offices in the country, and I'll be checking out a bit of trouble at the head office in La Paz. I have some friends in the city, the Evanses. They are a young missionary couple who work with the Quechua Indians, Bolivia's biggest ethnic group. The Quechua are direct descendants of the ancient Inca.

"My business in La Paz should only take a few hours, but I have some vacation time built up. I've been writing my friends in La Paz, and they've talked me into staying in Bolivia a couple of weeks for a real vacation."

"Boy, don't I wish I could go!" Justin exclaimed enviously. "I'm going to have a job just like yours someday, Uncle Pete, so I can see the world the way you do."

Jenny sighed. "It sounds so exciting. You'll take lots of pictures, won't you, Uncle Pete, especially of the Inca ruins? I'd love to see what they look like."

Uncle Pete grinned, looking suddenly like Justin when he was planning some mischief. "Well, as a matter of fact..." He glanced across the table at his brother, who mirrored his grin.

"Actually, I thought maybe you'd like to take your own pictures."

Jenny and Justin froze in their seats. "Do you mean?" they burst out in unison.

Uncle Pete looked apologetically at Mrs. Parker. "I hadn't meant to say anything until I had a chance to talk to you, Helen. Ron wrote that you wouldn't be able to take a family vacation this summer—with that big project Boeing is working on. With the kids out of school, I thought maybe they'd like to come along with me."

Mrs. Parker frowned, and Justin held his breath. He knew his mother didn't like surprises—and the two Parker men had a habit of springing surprises on her.

"I talked the idea over with Ron on the way here from the airport. He said he'd leave it up to you. It would be an educational experience for the children, and I'd really enjoy their company..."

"You don't know what kind of trouble these two can think up!" she protested. "Besides, they're too young to be traveling alone."

"They wouldn't be alone! I'd keep a good eye on them," Uncle Pete promised.

"I don't know..." Mrs. Parker said, still frowning. "This is a little sudden. I'll have to talk it over with Ron." She made the mistake of looking up into a circle of pleading eyes, and her expression softened.

"Well, I don't suppose anything can happen to

them with you along, Pete." Justin slowly let out his breath as his mother continued, "This *is* quite an opportunity. If you kids will promise to be careful and do everything your uncle tells you..."

She never got a chance to finish her sentence because Jenny was out of her chair and dancing around the table. Even Justin was quivering with excitement.

"Thanks, Mom! You won't be sorry!" Justin said. Jenny exuberantly hugged first her mother, then Uncle Pete, and finally her father. Whirling around the room, she chanted, "We're going to Bolivia! We're going to Bolivia!"

"Well, kids," Uncle Pete said in an amused tone, "I take it you're willing to come?" Their shining eyes alone would have been answer enough.

"Okay, Jenny, let's sit down," Uncle Pete commanded. As he pulled out a small notebook from his breast pocket, the twins were reminded that their favorite uncle was also a very capable business executive.

"We will be leaving three weeks from Saturday. In that time we'll need to get your passports, contact the nearest Bolivian consulate, and make travel reservations."

He fastened a stern eye on both children. "I'm allowing you only one suitcase apiece. You'll need warm clothing as well as a few lighter outfits. Bolivia lies south of the equator and, if you remember your geography, it's in the middle of winter right now. It isn't as cold as our northern winters, but it can get pretty chilly—especially since the buildings are unheated.

"Now I'm sure you've had all your vaccinations, but you'll need a few extra shots for traveling—yellow fever, typhoid, malaria..."

Jenny poked Justin in the ribs and whispered, "Did you hear that? Yuck! I can't stand shots!"

But Justin was listening with only half an ear. He was seeing visions of ancient golden cities; of haughty Indian warriors marching across a vast, brown plateau, bronze-tipped spears glittering under a deep-blue sky; of thousands of half-naked slaves hauling on giant blocks of granite, groaning under the cruel whip of their Inca overseer.

I'm not dreaming! he thought to himself in awe. *I'm really going. You, Justin Parker, are actually going to see the land of the mighty Incas!*